Obeying God

Obeying God

THE WAY TO THE FATHER'S HEART

MONICA BURNEY

XULON PRESS

Xulon Press
2301 Lucien Way #415
Maitland, FL 32751
407.339.4217
www.xulonpress.com

Paperback ISBN-13: 978-1-6312-9285-9
Ebook ISBN-13: 978-1-6312-9286-6

August 16, 2022

To the bookstore manager:

Back in November 2020, I sent your bookstore a copy of my newly published book, "Obeying God." As a first-time author, I was encouraged by the positive response I received from various sources. I submitted the book to my publisher for its annual Christian Author's Contest, and the book was awarded third place in the Christian Living category. I also have continued to receive numerous comments validating the book as a valuable discipleship tool, as well as a meaningful devotional book.

Since the first edition was published, I was able to have a professional editor edit the book. Additionally, it was suggested that I add study questions at the end of chapters, so that it can be used in leading Bible studies.

challenges and opportunities in their faith journey, as well as to encourage others in their faith walk.

I hope that you will take time to preview this updated version of the book and consider adding more copies of "Obeying God" to the selection you offer at your bookstore.

By His grace,

Monica Burney

Monica Burney

(707) 463-2092
burneyfam@prodigy.net
targettruthministries.com

TABLE OF CONTENTS

To my loving and gracious Father, who daily gives me new reasons to be thankful, humbled, and amazed by Your extravagant love. May my life reflect my gratitude and the blessed hope that is mine because of You.

I thank my precious husband, friend, and ministry partner, Gerry, for all the love and joy you bring to my life.

ACKNOWLEDGMENTS

Special thanks to:

DeLois, Lois, Marylyn, Linda, Brendan, and Paul for being my "eyes" when deep in the forest, I couldn't see through the trees.

INTRODUCTION

You have laid down precepts that are to be fully obeyed. Oh, that my ways were steadfast in obeying your decrees! Then I would not be put to shame when I consider all your commands. I will praise you with an upright heart as I learn your righteous laws.

Psalm 119:4-8

Our entire existence, as Christians—our commitment, our commission, and all that He commands of us, can be summarized under one primary purpose and goal: to glorify God. In order to glorify God, we must obey God. To obey God, we must maintain an intimate relationship with Him through: (1) ongoing communication with Him in prayer; (2) an ever-deepening understanding of and adherence to His Word; (3) worshipping Him; (4) serving Him; and (5) fellowshipping with His people—the Body of Christ.

Communion with God produces a transformation in our lives by which we are able to realize present hope and eternal joy. Not only that, but as we are transformed into His likeness day by day, we become more effective ministers of His gospel of truth. This results in our being used to help others in their spiritual journey, as they also become partakers of the same heavenly blessings—all to the glory of God.

In John 15:5, He emphatically states, "I am the vine; you are the branches...apart from me you can do nothing." As we abide in the Vine at deeper levels, we come to understand His will and His sovereign ways more easily and more clearly. As we do, we come to realize that even though we are given many more commands to obey than just the Greatest Commandment, the Great Commission, and the Ten Commandments, we should not be overwhelmed nor feel weighed down by the sheer volume of those commands. Rather, we are promised that when we faithfully obey these commands, we will experience more freedom, peace, and contentment than ever before.

There are actually 613 commands in the Bible. Many of them do not apply to the New Testament church, but a great many of them do. God tells us in 1 John 5:3, "This is love for God: to obey his commands. And his commands are not burdensome." Knowing our weaknesses, He assures us that just like the yoke placed on oxen, His yoke is intended to make things more bearable for us—not more burdensome (see Matt. 11:29-30). We do not serve a ruthless taskmaster who takes pleasure in making unreasonable demands, in fact, quite the opposite. Just as any parent worth their salt puts restrictions on their children for their own protection, our God does so (and even more so), with the purpose of providing ultimate protection, freedom, and blessing for His children.

His fervent desire is to see us lean wholly on Him, trusting Him to do the heavy lifting, so that His glory may be displayed for all those around us to see. He proved this by sending Jesus to the cross for our sins, and He continues to confirm this daily as we walk in faithful obedience to Him.

This book was born out of my being challenged by two very small, yet persistently convicting words in the Bible: "all" and "every." Verses such as "take *every* thought captive to make it obedient to Christ"[1] and "Love the Lord your God with *all* your heart and with *all* your soul and with *all* your strength"[2] give me pause, as I consider their sheer gravity and scope and also as I seek to apply them to my life in Christ (*emphasis mine*).

Other verses such as "Be holy, because I am holy"[3] and "Be perfect, therefore, as your heavenly Father is perfect"[4] also have gnawed at my inner core, in light of the stunning reality of how holy and perfect Jesus was when He walked the earth. In other words, as fully divine, yet fully human, He proved leading a sinless life in this fallen world *is* possible: One moment at a time—one thought at a time—one conversation at a time—one decision at a time.

However, although it can be hard for us to reconcile our sin nature with God's commands to be "holy" and "perfect," we are given some form of relief in other places in the Bible. Verses such as 2 Corinthians 4:16, Philippians 1:6, and 3:12 confirm that we will never fully attain perfection this side of heaven, due to our fallen nature. Additionally, God provides us with a wide array of biblical examples of victorious Christian living

---

[1] 2 Cor. 10:5.

[2] Deut. 6:5.

[3] 1 Pet. 1:16.

[4] Matt. 5:48.

through the testimonies of credible, albeit flawed, men and women of God.

You may be familiar with an analogy often offered to people who are struggling with an overwhelming task: "So, how do you eat an elephant?" The answer then quickly comes, "One bite at a time." Well, this imagery of eating an elephant has never been an appealing visual for me. So instead, I propose we use a more palatable image of an artist's blank canvas as we explore the premise of this book on how we are to obey *all* of His applicable commands.

In doing so, we should bear in mind that as ones who are now in Christ, we are a brand new creation (2 Cor. 5:17). Our slate has been wiped clean because Jesus took our sins upon Himself at the cross. At the point of our conversion, God declares us positionally righteous by the blood of Jesus, as we surrender our lives to Him (Isa. 1:18; 2 Cor. 5:21). However, we still sin.

This side of heaven, we are neither fully holy, nor wholly perfect. So the question instead becomes, "How does the blank canvas of a new believer's life become God's perfect, finished masterpiece?" The short answer is *obedience*—obedience in response to His extravagant gift of redeeming, transforming grace. The long answer is one brush stroke at a time—one thought at a time— one decision at a time and so forth, as mentioned previously. Only by the grace of God and His indwelling Holy Spirit sanctifying and strengthening us day by day, can we have any possibility of fulfilling what He has commanded. However, we also have a part in this.

We were given the gift of free will, meaning our own choices will dictate just how much freedom and transformation we will experience in Christ. We are directed in

Romans 12:2 to "be transformed by the renewing of our mind." Yes, God can change our heart, our mind—our very lives. However, we play an active role in our transformation by deciding each moment of every day to what extent we will yield, obey, and trust Him in our lives.

Initially, influenced by Herbert Lockyer's book series (including *All the Doctrines of the Bible* and *All the Angels of the Bible*), the working title of this book was originally *All the Commands of the Bible.* However, as the concept of this book was further developed, I came to a growing awareness that this book was not intended to be an exhaustive study of all the commands He has given to us. Rather, it is meant to: (1) be an overview of the commands God has given believers; (2) make a compelling defense for why our daily goal as believers must be to comply with each of these commands; and (3) offer a strategy for how to obey all of His commands without losing heart.

The apostle Paul compares a believer's walk in Christ to that of a race and, more specifically, a marathon race—not a sprint (Heb. 12:1-3). As you walk through these pages with me and continue on in your faith journey, may you be challenged and changed by a deeper desire to obey Him in all ways, for always, and finish strong when your race is done.

> *We know that we have come to know*
> *him if we obey his commands...if anyone*
> *obeys his word, God's love is truly made*
> *complete in him. This is how we know we*
> *are in him: Whoever claims to live in him*
> *must walk as Jesus did.*
> *1 John 2:3, 5-6*

PART 1

GOD'S HEART

CHAPTER 1

COVENANT LOVE

*Know therefore that the LORD your God
is God; he is the faithful God, keeping his
covenant of love to a thousand generations of
those who love him and keep his commands.*
Deuteronomy 7:9

God's heart is the epitome of a father's heart. A devoted father loves, sacrifices, gives, disciplines, and provides for the needs of his children. However, unlike any earthly father, God's love is perfect. He showed this perfect love when He offered His only Son, Jesus—who experienced an unimaginably painful death on the cross to pay for all of our sins. He has given His children the ultimate gifts of love, forgiveness, reconciliation, and eternal life. He disciplines us for the express purpose of transforming us into His likeness, in preparation for us to enter eternity in His holy presence. He also provides for all of our needs: spiritual, as well as emotional, relational, and practical needs—as only He can.

God's covenant with His people is as faithful, strong, and true as it was with the Israelites long ago. His children are His most beloved creation and triumphant joy. Yet because of their propensity for pleasing self over pleasing Him, He also continues to know the heartache of a loving father, grieving at the poor choices of His children as well.

Time and time again in the Bible we see evidence of God's people putting Him to the test by their dissatisfaction, doubts, and disobedience, even as He continues to deliver them from bondage and reveal His character—that of a loving, merciful, generous, and trustworthy Heavenly Father. Whether it is the Israelites complaining about the manna provided to them in the wilderness, godly leaders questioning His instructions to them, or New Testament followers who are still trying to live under the law rather than under grace, God's steadfast love for His children never wavers. He may be silent for a time, chastise, or even punish those who disobey Him, but He promises us that nothing will ever separate us from His everlasting love, no matter how much we disappoint Him (Rom. 8:38-39).

To me, one of the most striking passages in the Bible that highlights God's great love for and longsuffering with His rebellious people is found in Psalm 78:

> *The men of Ephraim...they did not keep*
> *God's covenant and refused to live by his*
> *law. They forgot what he had done.*
> *(vv. 9-11)*
>
> *He divided the sea and led them through*
> *He guided them with the cloud by day and*

with light from the fire all night. (vv. 13-14)

They continued to sin against him...They willfully put God to the test...(vv. 17-18)

He rained down manna for the people to eat. (v. 24)

They ate till they had more than enough. (v. 29)

In spite of all this, they kept on sinning; in spite of the wonders, they did not believe. (v. 32)

Time after time he restrained his anger and did not stir up his full wrath. (v. 38)

This passage chronicles the stubborn willfulness of His chosen people, the Israelites. Over and over again, they broke God's heart as they rebelled and continually put Him to the test. Despite their ungrateful and ungodly behavior, He repeatedly showed them mercy and forgiveness, even though it was completely undeserved.

It is so easy for us to want to sit in judgment of them and say, "Those stiff-necked Israelites! How could they be so unfaithful to such a loving and gracious Father?" But the truth of the matter is, when it comes right down to it, we can be just like them.

There are all kinds of ways that can be cited of how we ourselves disobey God. For example, we can be guilty at times of caving into a "performance" mindset

when it comes to pleasing God. We can be on a performance treadmill and get too busy doing for God and
forget that our number one priority must always be to
abide with God. Or, we may offend God and others by
possessing a self-righteous attitude. Yet when we have
the wrong priorities or motives, the end result is that
we miss out on the perfect peace and joy He offers, and
worse yet, we displease God. David Needham, in his
book *Birthright* reminds us, "God did not save us first
to use us, to get us to perform. No, he saved us to love
us, to keep on giving himself to us!"[5]

We may read our Bibles daily, pray often, attend
church regularly, and serve Him in ministry, but we
can never outdo God when it comes to faithfulness.
Even as we continually attempt to carry out His commands, we still may fail Him by our wrong attitudes,
deviating from His instructions, not staying in balance
with commitments, or by not staying in intimate fellowship with Him.

As we do make pleasing God our highest priority, we
find, as John Piper once observed, "God is most glorified in us when we are most satisfied in him."[6] When
we do keep Him first in our lives, He grants us endurance as well as points of rest on our journey toward
our ultimate sanctification.

The Bible is chock-full of examples of God's faithfulness to us. We would do well to regularly visit passages such as Job 38:4-41, Psalms 74:12-17, 107,
111, 136, and 146:5-10 to remind us of what a faithful

---

[5] David Needham, *Birthright,* (Multnomah Publishers, 1999), p. 166.

[6] Rick Warren, *The Purpose Driven Life,* quoting John Piper (Zondervan, 2002),
p. 56.

and awesome God we serve. Likewise, the Bible also contains numerous reminders of the unfaithfulness of God's children as they have repeatedly grieved His heart by their unruly behavior and actions.[7]

When I was recovering from surgery several years back, God used that period of time to severely break my heart over my own sins. It was a very painful yet liberating time for me, leading to a release of joy and hopefulness that I had not experienced to such a large degree in a long while.

It caused me to reflect back on Israel's cycle of failing to obey God and how it led to their bondage and sorrow. I found myself right there with those stubborn Israelites—wandering in my own desert of desolation, desiring God's favor, yet stubbornly refusing to fully yield to Him in all areas of my life. As exemplary of a life as I wanted to believe I was living, God was making me painfully aware of the pride, the selfishness, and the willfulness I still held in my heart. God was chastening me—not to shame me, but out of His deep, abiding covenant love for me. His desire was (and is) to cleanse me, free me, heal me, and transform me.

He was also reminding me, once again, of how He had chosen me, pursued me, sacrificed for me, and redeemed me. Finally, He was renewing my hope of one day being set free from the anguish of sin, pain, and death to abide in His glorious presence in heaven forever.

In remembering how flawed and willful we are as believers—how difficult we often can make it on ourselves to keep His covenant—it can be easy to give into defeat and despair. However, a key to focusing on living

---

[7] See Exod. 32; Isa. 31; Jer. 11:1-17; Hos. 6:4-10; Matt. 23:37-39; Rev. 2:1-7.

victoriously is found in the book *Intense Moments with the Savior,* as Ken Gire comments, "I've learned my strength is not found in how intensely I struggle...but in how completely I surrender."[8]

Of the seven covenants God specifies in His Word, the covenant with Moses (found in Deut. 11), is the only one that is conditional—His promise to bless His people was contingent on them keeping the Ten Commandments. He set the standard. His holiness demands full compliance. Half-hearted, partial obedience can never pass as acceptable by His standards.

Still, He is patient with us as He prepares us for our eternal future with Him. He knows while we live on earth, we are frail and feeble. He knows we will break His laws—and His heart. Yet He also knows that as His children, we have been set apart for a holy purpose. He tells us in 1 Peter 2:9:

> *But you are a chosen people, a royal priesthood, a holy nation, a people belonging to God, that you may declare the praises of him who called you out of darkness into his wonderful light.*

Under the New Covenant (Jer. 31:31-34), God has made an unconditional promise—one that is based on grace, not on the law. It is not a matter of trying hard enough or earning points for good behavior or time served. It's about our trusting that God has made a provision for us through the redeeming blood of Jesus,

---

[8] Weaver, *Having a Mary Heart in a Martha World,* quoting Ken Gire, *Intense Moments with the Savior,* 86 (Waterbrook Press, 2000), p. 204.

whereby we are cleansed of our sins and made righteous in the eyes of a holy God.

> *For it is by grace you have been saved,*
> *through faith—and this not of yourselves,*
> *it is the gift of God—not by works, so that*
> *no one can boast.*
> *Ephesians 2:8-9*

Either way—conditional or unconditional—when God makes a covenant promise, He keeps it. There is no changing His mind. There is no confusion as to what He means. On His end, His covenant is firm and for always.

On the other hand, for generations, God's people have not always taken His covenants seriously. They have balked. They have bargained. They have distorted. They have reneged. They have wanted all the blessings of a covenantal relationship, but at the same time, they have sought to meet God on their own terms.

It would be easy to try to put some distance between us and them, but "they" in the above statements might just as easily describe you and me, too. At times, we may try to complicate God's covenant of love by making it more about us and our rights, rather than about Him and what He so rightly demands. Or, we may try to find "loopholes" in the agreement. However, His love, provision, and protection give us all the incentive in the world we need to keep our comparatively miniscule end of the bargain.

God's covenant love is not based on anything special that we have done. It is not based on our deserving His love. In our fallen state, we were destined for eternal separation from our Creator. Thankfully, He provided a way for us to be reconciled to Him through His Son Jesus. We are adopted into His family by His unrelenting grace and mercy.

We have only begun to experience the unfathomable riches of His great covenant love for us. The best is still yet to come.

> *I have loved you with an everlasting love.*
> *Jeremiah 31:3*

1a. What does the word "covenant" mean to you? Look up the following words in a dictionary:

Covenant –

Promise –

Vow –

1b. How are their meanings different from one another? How are they similar? Do any of the words carry more weight than the other two?

2. How does your awareness of God's covenantal love
    for His children influence your obedience to Him?

3. Read 1 Peter 2:9. What responsibilities do you bear
    as a member of God's "royal priesthood"?

CHAPTER 2

FELLOWSHIP

*God, who has called you into fellowship
with his Son Jesus Christ our Lord, is
faithful.*

1 Corinthians 1:9

When God created Adam and Eve, it was not out of need, but for His good pleasure. When they disobeyed Him, being the holy, all-powerful God that He is, He could easily have elected to annihilate them. However, being the merciful and loving God that He is, He instead punished them by banishing them from Eden—allowing them to suffer toil, pain, and death, but also making a way for them to be restored to Him for all eternity one day.

In Noah's time, when evil ran rampant due to corruption in the human seed (Gen. 6:1-8), God could have wiped out the entire human race. However, even though Noah and his family were not perfect, God spared them as a remnant, because, "Noah was a just man and perfect in his generations."[9] In other words, his bloodline was not corrupted, and through it, he would continue the human race so that at the appointed time, Jesus could fulfill God's plan to offer salvation to the world.

When Abraham sired Ishmael, God's permissive will allowed for a child not of covenant seed to be born. The birth of this child would prove to have long-ranging ramifications that continue to impact our world today. However, God's perfect will made it possible for Isaac to be born, thereby, continuing the covenant bloodline that would usher in the Messiah.

On Mt. Sinai, when Moses interceded on behalf of his people, God (fed up with the ingratitude and willful disobedience of His people), once again, showed mercy and withheld severest judgment by not completely destroying the entire multitude.[10]

God's track record for being both forgiving and faithful to keep His covenant promises are very evident to those who have been the grateful recipients of these and many of His other extraordinary blessings. However, despite our welcome relief and ever-deepening understanding of His patience, compassion, mercy, and love, 0we still continue to test Him sorely by our doubts and through our disobedience. Skeptical questions surface about God's trustworthiness in a variety of life situations that may occur, such as:

How could God let my baby die?

---

[9] Gen. 6:9.

[10] Deut. 9:12-29; 10.

Why must I always struggle so hard to make ends meet?

When will years of praying for my husband's salvation be answered?

Why must I keep serving so faithfully when I am so burned out and while so many around me are doing nothing to contribute to growing the kingdom of God?

How can I possibly forgive someone who continues to wound me so deeply?

These, and a plethora of other haunting questions, can plague the hearts and minds of believers, even as we profess a rock-solid faith in our sovereign God. We accept that God's nature is holy and perfect. We trust that what He says in His Word about Himself and about His love for us is absolute truth. Yet we doubt. We get discouraged. We may even get disillusioned at times, but we are in fine company as we consider the familiar testimonies of great men of God, such as Elijah and Job. As we will clearly see, even though God's heart is always to see His children trusting and obeying Him more fully, His primary motivation for such benevolence is fellowship with His creation.

Let us first look into the life of Elijah and then we will visit the land of Uz (not to be confused with the land of Oz!), where we will meet up with a very beleaguered Job.

In the case of Elijah, we see God's faithfulness to him as He ministers to him in his disillusioned state. After Elijah has valiantly stood against Baal's 450 false prophets, boldly beseeching the Lord to show His power and authority over the people so they might revere Him once again, God shows up in a mighty way. He not only brings fire down which consumes the sacrifice offered (along with the wood), but it also consumes the stones, the soil—even the water poured out over it all! When the people acknowledge God's sovereignty, they are then instructed to kill all of the false prophets.

Afterwards, King Ahab goes to Jezebel and reports to her of how all the prophets of Baal have been slaughtered. In her wrath, she makes a vow to avenge their deaths by ordering that Elijah be killed.

At this news, Elijah is overcome by fear and flees to Beersheba, where he finds shelter under a broom (juniper) tree. He is weary and worn from the fight. He is fearful and despairing even of life, as he pleads with the Lord to take his life.

Although it would appear that Elijah was at his lowest point, God already had a plan in place to further use him for kingdom purposes. He did not deem him a failure, nor did He give up on him. He saw his frailty, but desiring to refresh Elijah physically and restore him spiritually, he sent an angel to minister to him (my paraphrase of 1 Kings 19).

And so it is with us. Whether we are in the thick of a spiritual battle involving others, or we struggle within ourselves, we are reminded that our God fights for us. He goes before us. He walks beside us and He has put His Spirit within our hearts to guide us. As with Elijah, He finds creative ways to remind us that the battle belongs to Him.[11] He promises to never leave us or forsake us. And as we submit to His will, relying on Him

---

[11] 1 Sam. 17:47.

to meet our every need, He draws us nearer to Him and we get a glimpse of the sweet, unfiltered fellowship that Adam and Eve experienced with Him in Paradise.

We need to daily surrender *fully* to His will and His authority over our lives, trusting that He will ultimately work it all out for our benefit and for His glorious name. Easy—right? Truthfully, it seems more a case of easier said than done. Still, it *is* doable... one deliberate choice after another to walk humbly, faithfully, and obediently.

As we take a look into the life of Job, we find a man who is richly blessed as he faithfully seeks after God:

> *In the land of Uz there lived a man whose name was Job. This man was blameless and upright; he feared God and shunned evil. He had seven sons and three daughters, and he owned seven thousand sheep, three thousand camels, five hundred yoke of oxen and five hundred donkeys, and had a large number of servants. He was the greatest man among all the people of the East.*
>
> *Job 1:1-3*

His life is humming along until he experiences a series of devastating calamities, which are sanctioned by God, but perpetrated by Satan: Job's ten children are killed, his livestock destroyed, and nearly all of his servants have also perished (vv. 13-19). Job's response displays his steadfastness of heart by saying:

> *Naked I came from my mother's womb, and naked I will depart. The LORD gave and*

*the LORD has taken away; may the name
of the LORD be praised. (v. 21)*

Job then endures yet another round of severe testing as he is stricken with sores all over his body, from head to toe. To add to his misery, his wife and three friends are anything but supportive and it all begins to take a toll on him:

*What strength do I have, that I should still
hope? (6:11)*

*If I have sinned, what have I done to you, O
watcher of men? Why have you made me
your target? Have I become a burden to
you? (7:20)*

As he engages back and forth with his friends long and hard (while also wrestling with God and himself), he finally makes peace with the situation. Coming to terms with his human limitations and acknowledging God's sovereignty, he exclaims:

*'I know you can do all things; no plan of
yours can be thwarted. You asked, Who
is this that obscures my counsel without
knowledge?' surely I spoke of things I did
not understand, things too wonderful for
me to know.' (42:2-3)*

So what are we to derive from this extreme example of God allowing one of His own to be so severely tested? Is He a cruel, harsh, unloving Father? Does He take delight in seeing His children suffer? If He has the power to prevent calamities or pain of any kind, why doesn't He?

Despite how things may appear, God's deepest desire is to have intimate, unbroken fellowship with His children. The great sacrifice He made to save us should remove any doubt in our minds about how much He loves us and wants the very best for our lives. Because He is a holy and perfect God, He allows us to endure trials, testing, discipline, and hardship in order to prepare us for the glories of heaven.

Unlike us, Jesus, the perfect Son of God, did not need to be sanctified. The secret to Jesus' fulfilling His earthly mission with such complete submission, despite the extraordinary challenges He faced, was to abide in the Vine—allowing nothing to detract or deter him from fellowship with His Father. This continual feasting of fellowship is what allowed Him to embrace His role and fulfill His most difficult tasks with utter joy and deliberateness.[12] We are also called to abide in the Vine and enjoy continual fellowship with our Father.

When we become a Christ-follower, we are asked to deny ourselves and to take up our cross daily.[13] Like Paul, we must learn to embrace suffering as an opportunity to, "know Christ and the power of his resurrection and the fellowship of sharing in his sufferings" (Phil. 3:10).

We are told in 1 John 5:19 that, "the whole world is under the control of the evil one." One day, the enemy of our souls will be destroyed and we will forever be free of his schemes to, "steal, kill and destroy" (John 10:10). For now, however, even when our struggles do

---

[12] Heb. 12:2.

[13] Luke 9:23.

come by way of the enemy, God is the only One who has the final say of what trials enter into our lives. He is still sovereign over all.

Whatever the enemy means for evil, God will use for good in our lives: If we stand firm on His statutes. If we don't waver. When we remember who is on the throne. As we reflect on what a mighty and merciful God we serve. And, as we rejoice that the Creator of the universe—the Great I AM—is the Lover of our souls and takes great pleasure in our companionship.

1. Define the word "blameless." Besides Job (see Job 1:1), what other examples can you find in the Bible of someone being viewed by God as blameless?

2. Read 1 Thess. 5:23-24. How else can this prayer of blessing be viewed? As a promise? A goal? An expectation?

3. Look up the following verses: Psalm 15:2-3, Psalm 119:1, Philippians 2:14-16a, and James 3:2. How are we to become "blameless"?

CHAPTER 3

SACRIFICE

For God so loved the world that he gave his one and only Son, that whoever believes in him shall not perish but have eternal life.
John 3:16

In light of our Father's pure, holy, and perfect loving heart we recognize that:

- He *has* done His part, by sending Jesus, the perfect model for humanity and the perfect sacrifice for our sins.
- He *is doing* His part by continuing to renew the hearts and minds of those who are His.
- He *will do* His part by sending His Son to return to earth, to destroy evil once and for all and to take His children home to live with Him forever one day soon.

His ways are so much higher than our ways.[14] What He offers us is so far above and beyond what He ever expects from us. Not only has He given us His Son Jesus, but He has also given us the Holy Spirit and His Word.

The Greatest Gift—Jesus Christ
(2 Corinthians 9:15)

> *For you know the grace of our Lord Jesus Christ, that though he was rich, yet for your sakes he became poor, so that you through his poverty might become rich.*
>
> *2 Corinthians 8:9*

Before Jesus ever died on the cross, He had already sacrificed and endured so incredibly much to fulfill His Father's plan of redemption for us. Most amazingly, He left the glories of heaven to come into a broken, filthy, sin-stained world. Secondly, in the three years of His public ministry, He was ridiculed, threatened, despised, slandered, plotted against, unjustly accused, denied a fair trial, brutally beaten, and imprisoned. Thirdly, He spent much of His last night on earth praying alone in utter anguish, before being arrested, tried, convicted, mocked, and beaten. Finally, the next day, He made the excruciating trek to Calvary, carrying a cross as no one else ever has or ever will have to carry.

Then, bearing the weight of the sinfulness of all mankind, enduring physical pain beyond comprehension, and experiencing isolation from His Father for

---

[14] Isa. 55:9.

a moment in time, He cried out, "My God, my God, why have you forsaken me?" In His final act of obedience to His Father while in human form, our sinless Savior died on Calvary's hill, having completed His earthly mission.

> The Gospel says you are more sinful and
> flawed than you ever dared believe, yet you
> are more accepted and loved than you ever
> dared hope because Jesus lived and died
> in your place.[15]

The Gift of the Holy Spirit:

> *And hope does not disappoint us, because*
> *God has poured out his love into our hearts*
> *by the Holy Spirit, whom he has given us.*
> *Roman 5:5*

Along with the gift of Jesus, our precious Savior, God has also given us His Holy Spirit. In the book of John, chapters 14 and 16, we are told of the Counselor, the Spirit of truth, "who will teach [us] all things" and "guide [us] into all truth" (vv. 14:26, 16:13).

Additionally, in Acts 1:8, we are assured power through the Holy Spirit. This supernatural power source makes it possible for us to tear down strongholds, boldly witness to the lost, and be victorious in fulfilling our God-given purpose on earth.

When the disciples walked with Jesus, they sat under His teachings, observed His heart of compassion

---

[15] Pete Scazzero, *The Emotionally Healthy Church* (Zondervan, 2003), p. 81

and humble manner of ministering, and witnessed many of His miracles. After Jesus returned to His heavenly throne, He sent them the Holy Spirit, as He had promised. At Pentecost, once they had received the Holy Spirit, the disciples saw another promise come to fruition, as they were able to do even greater works than Jesus[16] by exponentially expanding the kingdom—having immediately added three thousand on that very special day alone.[17]

As we grow deeper in our knowledge of this precious gift and become more closely attuned to God's will and His ways, His power is made more strongly manifested in us. It's not automatic. We need to constantly "keep in step with the Spirit" (Gal. 5:25), in order to receive the full benefit of His residing within us. In tandem with this, we must continually work to keep our hearts, our minds, and our bodies (the temple of the Holy Spirit), completely free of contamination. What a blessed and awesome task is ours!

Those who walk intimately in the Spirit come to greatly value this member of the Trinity who "helps our weakness" and "intercedes for *us* with groanings too deep for words."[18] He is our Comforter, our Guide, and our Intercessor. Yet among His prominent purposes, He also exists to "convict the world of guilt in regard to sin."[19] It is by His prompting that human hearts awaken to their depravity and their need for a Savior.

---

[16] John 14:12.

[17] Acts 2:41

[18] Rom. 8:26 (NASB).

[19] John 16:8.

The Gift of God's Word:

*For the word of God is living and active
Sharper than any double-edged sword,
it penetrates even to dividing soul and spirit,
joints and marrow; it judges the thoughts
and attitudes of the heart.*

Hebrews 4:12

As if these extravagant gifts weAre not enough, He has also imparted His very Word to us, divinely inspired, to speak truth into our lives. He tells us in Romans 15:4: "For everything that was written in the past was written to teach us so that through endurance and the encouragement of the Scriptures we might have hope." This verse gives us assurance that God understands the frailties and feebleness of the human condition. By speaking to us directly through His divine Word, He has provided a way for us to navigate through all of the complexities of living in this fallen world in a way that works to our benefit and brings glory to Him and His kingdom.

His Word is flawless and forever. His Word does not return to Him void. His Word is right and true. In His Word we find light and life. It is our sword to combat the lies and deceptions of the enemy. It is our daily bread. As we observe in Matthew 4, Jesus gave us a picture of this as He fasted in the desert for forty days and nights, while facing the temptations of the enemy.

Although fully divine, His body (in human form) experienced the physical symptoms from extreme hunger by the end of His time in the desert. However, He was sustained not only physically, but also spiritually, when deflecting Satan's arrows with the truth of God's Holy Word and then receiving aid from God's ministering angels.

When we grow faint (whether suffering a physical trial, emotional upheaval, or spiritual battle), one of the quickest ways to find strength, comfort, and hope is to hold fast to the Scriptures. This is why He tells us not to just merely read, but also memorize, meditate on, study, even pray the Scriptures. It gives us strength for the journey. Not only does it fortify our faith personally, but it emboldens us to share our faith with others. It has power to extinguish the fiery darts from the enemy and it draws us ever closer to God.

With God's statutes and powerful testimonies found in His Word to guide us, the Holy Spirit convicting our hearts, and Jesus' perfect example of a sinless life to challenge and encourage us, we have been given all we need to walk a life of total obedience and in eternal blessedness with God.

At the core of all three of these gifts is His gift of love, found in forms of forgiveness, grace, mercy, joy, peace, wisdom, and so much more. It would take volumes to describe all of these in depth, however, in coming chapters, we will look at some highlights of each. Next, we will look at one more aspect of God's heart: Justice.

1. Read 2 Corinthians 8:9, Philippians 2:5-8, and Matthew 5:3. In view of Jesus' poverty ("making himself nothing" for our sakes), how are we to become spiritually "impoverished?"

2. What affect does our becoming "spiritually impoverished" have on others? Does it achieve a kingdom purpose? If so, what might it achieve?

3. Think about specific times you can recall that the Holy Spirit guided you in a significant way. When these times have occurred, have you shared with others how He guided you? In what ways have you hindered the work of the Holy Spirit in the past?

CHAPTER 4

JUSTICE

The Lord loves righteousness and justice.
Psalm 33:5

Another aspect of God's fatherly attributes is seen in His heart for justice. Any good father who sees his children in pain, suffers along with them, and will do anything humanly possible to ease their pain. And, if they are in danger, he is willing to risk his very life for them.

Our God, in His great mercy, sent His only Son as a substitute to take our place and rescue us from eternal damnation. That said, many people still cannot begin to understand how God could allow so much suffering to occur in this world. The question is often raised, "If He is such a loving God and He is all-powerful, why doesn't He intervene in human tragedies?" This very question was raised at Calvary as scornful onlookers shouted out to Jesus, "You who are going to destroy the temple and build it in three days, save yourself! Come down from the cross, if you are the Son of God!"[20]

Although every bit of suffering that occurs in this world has God's permission, He does not cause all of it. This is an important distinction to make, since so many people are so quick to blame God for every tragedy. While it is true that some pain or anguish can be directly linked to consequences, as a result of sinful behavior (such as Jonah being swallowed by the giant fish), not every circumstance involving pain is a result of sin or God's wrath.

In John 9:1-3, the disciples query Jesus about whether the blindness of the man He heals was caused due to sin by the man or by his parents. Jesus responds that it was not due to any sin, but only "that the work of God might be displayed in his life" (v.3). This was also true in the story of Job. Although God will often use painful circumstances to shape our character, increase our faith, and draw us nearer to His presence, it is never with the intent to be cruel or arbitrary. In fact, He tells us in Jeremiah 29:11, "His plan is not to harm us, but to give us a hope and a future."

It is the enemy, "the thief who comes to steal, kill and destroy"[21] who means to harm us. John 16:11 assures us that Satan ("the prince of this world") is already condemned. The victory was won when Jesus died and rose again. However, until the final battle, when Satan is finally and fully destroyed, the earth is

---

[20] Matt. 27:40.

[21] John 10:10.

still his domain.[22] For now though, we can rest in the full knowledge that God is completely in control.

When Satan set out to test Job, he could only do so with God's consent. After Joseph had endured many hardships (initiated at the hand of his brothers' sinful actions), he came to recognize that what they "meant for evil against [him], God meant...for good in order to bring about this present result, to preserve many people alive."[23]

When God sees one of His beloved children suffering, He is deeply grieved and is full of compassion—even when it is the result of the necessary consequences of sin. But when that suffering comes by way of evil, His sense of justice ensures that the evildoer will suffer a far worse fate in the end. In this age of our witnessing rampant evil, such as mass shootings, human trafficking, abuse, drug and alcohol epidemics, and gang violence, we can take comfort in His assurances found in passages such as Deuteronomy 32:35 and Proverbs 11:21. His vengeance is sure. He will not let any evil deed go unpunished. The battle belongs to the Lord[24]

Even though God fights for us (and He is the only One who can ultimately vanquish the enemy), He also enlists us to be warriors in the fight against evil: to boldly make a stand for truth, to pray down the strongholds, and to confront darkness with the light of God's love. In this fight, we can know that we have the full power of God's unlimited resources at our disposal. We can put on our spiritual armor, confident that we are

---

[22] 1 John 5:19.

[23] Gen. 50:20 (NASB).

[24] 1 Sam. 17:47.

fully equipped to meet the enemy—just as David was fully armed as he met the giant with only a sling and some stones. As conflicts and confrontations arise, we need to remember that we are fighting not "against flesh and blood," as Ephesian 6:12 warns us, but "against the dark world and against the spiritual forces of evil in the heavenly realms."

God supplies all that we need. We cannot fight in our own strength. We are admonished that in order to ensure victory, we must "be strong in the Lord and in his mighty power" (Eph. 6:10). The enemy is a loathsome foe, but he is no match for God's arsenal of heavenly power and authority. God's justice always prevails.

Later on, we will explore further all that is expected of us as we do our part. Next, we will examine the precious gifts and promises God has given us, that clearly show us His heart of love toward us and how they demonstrate the costly sacrifice His part requires.

1. Look up the word "justice" in a dictionary. Given it's meaning, what distinctions can be made between man's justice and God's justice?

2. Read Micah 6:8. Give some specific examples from the Bible that show what God intends when He commands us "to do justice."

3. In an age where people are concerned about justice more than ever, as a believer, how can you live out God's command "to do justice"?

PART 2

GOD'S PART

CHAPTER 5

FORGIVENESS

*If we confess our sins, he is faithful and
just and will forgive us our sins and purify us
from all unrighteousness.*

1 John 1:9

U nlike humans, God is not capable of doing anything halfway. It is all or nothing with Him. Now
that can be a real comfort or a real curse, depending
on who you are. If you believe in Him, no problem: for
He saves you, justifies you, adopts you, loves you, forgives you, and sanctifies you—completely. Conversely,
if you deny Him, you've got big problems, as not only
will He deny you all the joys and privileges of His covenant blessings including: the comfort of His presence,
the love of Jesus, the power of His Holy Spirit, the guidance of His Word, along with the provision and protection He gives, but you will also be denied the hope of
eternal life in glory.

God stands at the ready to forgive us and cleanse
us from *all* of our sins. However, being the holy, sovereign God that He is, He must also completely cut off

those who are unwilling to receive His offer of forgiveness. He created us. He gave us free will. He paid a high price to provide us the opportunity to be restored to relationship with Him. He gets to set the boundaries. It's all—or nothing.

When we are saved, He justifies us at that very first moment. He sees us as wholly righteous, and this, made possible only by the atoning blood of Jesus. Yet as fallen humans, we still continue to sin and therefore, still need to daily confess our sins and receive His forgiveness.

His promise to us to not only forgive us fully, but also to completely forget our sins is remarkable when we consider how hard it is for us to forgive others, much less forget when they have wronged us in some way. He tells us in Psalm 103:12, "As far as the east is from the west so far has he removed our transgressions from us."

While we can be guilty of whining, complaining, withholding, vacillating, and making excuses of why we can't forgive someone, He does not hesitate, even for a second, to forgive us our every transgression when we confess and repent—no matter how egregious the sin. Then, He goes one step further by wiping the sin entirely from His memory.

Jesus gave us the ultimate example of God's forgiveness. Dying on the cross, He not only suffered excruciating physical pain, but also the cruelty of the taunting soldiers and onlookers, bearing the shame as they hurled insults at Him. His response was extraordinary as He asked God to forgive them (Luke 23:34). Likewise, God the Father was extending forgiveness to those putting His beloved Son to death. Jesus the Son, in His final moments on earth, interceded on behalf of those who falsely accused Him, beat and tortured Him, ridiculed Him, and nailed Him to a cross. Can we do no less than the same—to show mercy and offer forgiveness to those who have offended us for far lesser offenses?

In Matthew 6:14-15, we are told that if we forgive others when they sin against us, He will forgive us—unequivocally. However, He also warns us that if we do not forgive them their offense toward us, then our sins will not be forgiven. Potent words from a just God.

I once had a friend who was very precious to me. I met her at a time when she was in crisis. We shared a lot in common and we shared a lot of really fun and meaningful times together. One day, the friendship abruptly ended, with no explanation on her part. At first, I was deeply hurt. Then I was angry that she would not share with me how I might have offended her, so that we could reconcile. After awhile, although I missed our friendship, I moved on—or so I thought.

After some time had passed, she tried contacting me several times. She wanted back into my life. Although I believed I had truly forgiven her, I wasn't sure I could trust her and so I did not respond. However, not long after this, I ran into her several times within a period of a week or so and determined that God was trying to tell me something. So I contacted her and we reconciled—for a time. It was a pleasant reunion, she told me that I had, in fact, offended her, but that she came to realize it was purely unintentional. We went on to make several more sweet memories together.

Then, to my dismay, it happened again. She abruptly ended the friendship, citing she was going through something and basically just needed her space.

As painful as it was to lose this friend a second time, God showed me that the Bible verses I have memorized are only as meaningful as the degree to which I apply them to my life. He brought to my mind Peter's noble-sounding questions (found in Matthew 18:21-22), as to how many times he should forgive his brother, to which Jesus responds with an answer that demonstrates just how much fallen humans still have to learn about forgiveness. More to the point, it convicted me of how far I personally miss the mark in light of Jesus' love, forgiveness, and humility.

In conceptualizing the meaning of Micah 7:19 for her own life, Corrie ten Boom once remarked, "Why should I hold onto the sins of others while my own sins have been cast into the depths of the sea?" As believers, this is a vitally important truth to grasp. I know it has redirected my thought path many times, as I myself have had to concede to the profound reality that I am a sinner—albeit a sinner saved by grace, but still, a sinner.

As a flawed, sinful person, I must recognize and make allowances for others' flawed, sinful nature. If I, who have already been the recipient of so much undeserved grace and mercy, hope to have continued forgiveness extended to me for all my many transgressions, I must also be willing to extend forgiveness to others for theirs.

Time and again, we've heard stories of giants of the faith bearing testimony to the goodness of God through the power of forgiveness. Joseph forgave his brothers after they threw him in a pit, sold him into slavery, and told their father that he was dead. David, betrayed by his mentor, King Saul, forgave him—even knowing that

Saul was out to kill him. More modern-day examples come to mind such as Corrie ten Boom (*The Hiding Place*) and Louis Zamperini (*Unbroken*), who forgave their captors and tormentors. More recently, Bart Millard's story of forgiving an abusive father also gives compelling evidence of the power of forgiveness.[25]

We are without excuse. We are assured that "we are *more than* conquerors"[26] who can "do *all* things through Christ who gives us strength"[27]—including forgiving both friends and our foes (*emphasis mine*).

It is amazing just how fully God forgives us and how incredibly much it cost Him to make that forgiveness possible. Yet we still continue to disappoint Him by our stubborn, rebellious, and self-righteous behavior. May all praise be to our gracious Father for the gift of forgiveness and the miracle of His grace.

1. Read Psalm 103:12 and Isaiah 44:22. How does knowing that God has forgiven and forgotten your sins influence your willingness to forgive others?

---

[25] Bart Milard, *I Can Only Imagine* (Lionsgate/Erwin Brothers Entertainment, 2018).

[26] Rom. 8:37.

[27] Phil. 4:13.

2. If God has already forgiven all of our sins (Col. 3:13), why do we need to confess our sins and ask Him for forgiveness (1 Jn. 1:1-9)?

3. Are there any valid reasons you can think of for withholding forgiveness from someone who has wronged you? If so, what Scripture references can you cite as justification?

CHAPTER 6

GRACE

*For the grace of God that brings salvation
has appeared to all men. It teaches us to
say "No" to ungodliness and worldly
passions, and to live self-controlled, upright
and godly lives in this present age, while
we wait for the blessed hope—the glorious
appearing of our great God and Savior,
Jesus Christ, who gave himself for us to
redeem us from all wickedness and to
purify for himself a people that are his
very own, eager to do what is good.*

Titus 2:11-14

The apostle Paul is a great one to teach us on the topic of God's grace. After all, previously (as Saul), he was an enemy of Christians—and therefore, an enemy of the theology of grace. Mercifully, God radically changed his heart to such an extent that he went on to become one the most notable recipients of grace and one of its most boldest messengers. In fact, Paul was so painfully aware of how much God had forgiven him and extended grace to him that he even went so far as to say that he was the "chief of all sinners" (1 Tim. 1:15).

In addition to his deeply heavy and penitent heart over his past transgressions (namely, being responsible for the brutal persecution of scores of Christians), he also came to understand grace in the context of his own personal hardships—whether it be the thorn in the flesh he refers to in 2 Corinthians 12:7 or the myriad of other forms of suffering he experienced and recounts in 2 Corinthians 11:23-28.

In the midst of his trials, he comes to know full well the blessed reality and benefit of God's assurance: that God's grace is indeed sufficient (2 Cor. 12:9), as he willingly suffers severely for the cause of Christ. He views fully surrendering his will to God's as the only reasonable response he could give to the incredible grace and mercy God had shown him initially, as well as God's ongoing lavishing of grace upon his life as he faced trials and temptations. Even as he does plead with God three times to have the unspecified "thorn" removed from him, he comes to a place of acceptance, learning "to be content whatever the circumstances" (Phil. 4:11).

How many of us can honestly boast such a statement? To say that we are completely content, no matter what we are going through, is exactly where God wants us to be. However, the path to get us there is replete with painful lessons and difficult tests. Most assuredly, it is not for the foolhardy or the fainthearted.

Maintaining this attitude at all times requires an inordinate amount of humility, along with a life-long procession of praise and thanksgiving: in times of abundance and in times of need, in times of fear and in times of hope, in times of pain and in times of pleasure.

Horatio Spafford (1828-1888) is best known for penning the words to the beloved hymn "It is Well with My Soul." He wrote this song as he journeyed across the ocean to join his wife, Anna, after the loss of their four daughters, who were lost at sea. The depth of his pain is unimaginable. Yet because of his deep faith, steeped in the sufficiency of God's grace, he could write with absolute conviction:

> When peace, like a river, attendeth my
> way, when sorrows like sea billows roll;
> whatever my lot, thou hast taught me to say,
> It is well, it is well with my soul.[28]

For many, responding to adversity in such a fashion may seem incomprehensible, if not impossible. It can be so much easier to let the pain lead us away from God in bitter dismay, rather than to lean hard on the Comforter, allowing His grace to cover us and His perfect peace to soothe our aching hearts.

The secret to Paul's success as a true believer and as an effective minister of the gospel was in his keeping his focus squarely fixed upon His gracious Savior. By keeping such a laser focus, he achieved a tremendous depth of understanding of God's grace at work in his own life, as well as recognizing the immense need of this gift of grace for every individual.

To receive God's gift of grace is extremely humbling. It is also absolutely liberating. When we truly grasp

---

[28] Horatio Spafford, *It Is Well With My Soul (Public domain)*.

the gravity of what Jesus endured on the cross for us and just how undeserving we are, we can join Paul in saying, "May I never boast except in the cross of our Lord Jesus Christ" (Gal. 6:14). And, as we are empowered to meet our challenges head on, we do well to remember the unmerited favor bestowed upon us as His beloved children and as we continue to acknowledge and testify to His amazing grace in every moment of our lives.

God's grace is a free gift, but it is also a costly gift. Even though there is nothing we can do to earn it, once we've received it, we reap not only huge benefits from it, but we also bear some responsibility in receiving it. The benefits are extravagant and everlasting:

> *And God is able to make all grace abound*
> *to you, so that in all things at all times,*
> *having all that you need, you will abound*
> *in every good work.*
> *2 Corinthians 9:8*

The responsibility that comes with receiving God's grace is to bear witness to the gift and to the Giver by being a mirror of His radiant reflection.

> *The grace of God in the heart of man is*
> *a tender plant in a strange unkindly soil.*
> *Robert Leighton*
> (from *Intimate Faith* by Jan Winebrenner)

1. In 2 Corinthians 12:9, Paul states that God's "grace is sufficient for you" and that His "power is made perfect in weakness." Think of a situation in which you clearly knew that God was covering you with His grace. In retelling of that situation to others, how would you explain the manifestation of His grace? How would you describe how His power" is made perfect in weakness" to others?

2. Read Colossians 4:6. What is meant by Paul's statement with regard to how our conversations should be "always full of grace" and "seasoned with salt"?

3. How can we "grow in the grace and knowledge of our Lord and Savior Jesus Christ" (2 Pet. 3:18)?

4. How does 2 Corinthians 9:8 give us full assurance that God's grace is enough to meet our every need, challenge, and assignment in this life?

CHAPTER 7

MERCY

His mercy is great.

2 Samuel 24:14

U nlike grace (receiving that which is undeserved), mercy withholds that which is completely deserved. As it pertains to the sinfulness of fallen mankind, it is God's withholding His just punishment of eternal separation from Him from those who have believed in His Son and, subsequently, are reconciled to Him, justified by Christ's righteousness.

However, just like grace, this gift is bestowed out of compassion from a Heavenly Father whose very nature is extravagant love—untainted by any misdirected motives.

In the parable of the unmerciful servant (Matt. 18:21-35), Jesus paints a portrait of mercy along with a contrast—showing also that which is unmerciful. He tells of how a certain servant owes his king more money than he could ever repay. When the king is made aware of this, he first orders that the servant and his entire family be sold to repay the debt. However, in desperation the servant cries out for mercy and the king, feeling compassion for him, forgives the entire debt.

Now you would think that the servant would be full of gratitude, recognizing how the king's generosity vastly improved the quality of his life (and that of his family), for the better. Instead, when given the opportunity to pay it forward to a fellow servant (who owed him a much smaller debt and was now imploring him to forgive his debt), he shows no mercy whatsoever.

The king then gets wind of this travesty and orders the unmerciful servant to be thrown in jail, demanding that he pay back the enormous debt he had just previously been forgiven.

When I think about my life and of all the many times I've been made keenly aware of how much God has forgiven my sins (and just how completely unworthy I am to receive such forgiveness), it is inconceivable to me that I would ever hesitate to dispense mercy to others when it is needed. And yet, I can point to a number of occasions when I somehow was blinded by my own pride, hurt, or anger, and withheld mercy from another.

In the moment, a lack of mercy can appear to be defensible in certain situations. In retrospect, we hopefully come to realize it is inexcusable. However, both the challenge and goal is to remember, while still in the moment, that our unmerciful acts are always indefensible.

In the case of the adulterous woman who was not stoned (John 8:1-11), her accusers abandoned their mission to stone her to death because Jesus skillfully brought to their awareness their own sinfulness, and they were then judiciously convicted in their hearts. The woman also was convicted in her heart in that moment, and immediately turned away from her sinful lifestyle.

In addition to the story of the adulterous woman, Jesus gives us a slightly different aspect of mercy in His illustration in Luke 7:36-50. When questioned by Simon the Pharisee as to why Jesus would allow a sinful woman entrance to the dinner party at Simon's house, Jesus helps Simon gain some perspective. He first tells a story of two men indebted to a third man. He states that one owes him more than the other. He draws Simon in further by telling him that the moneylender canceled both of their debts. He then asks Simon his opinion as to which debtor was more grateful. Simon answers correctly, stating that the one who was forgiven more was the more grateful one. Jesus then connects the dots for Simon, showing the parallel between the sinful woman and Simon in their treatment of Jesus. They are both indebted to Jesus, but it is the sinful woman who displays the most love, respect, and gratitude to Him.

In John 8, the adulterous woman demonstrated she was more grateful than her accusers, evidenced by her genuine repentance and radically changed life. In Luke 7, the sinful woman who anointed Jesus' feet with perfume and wiped His feet with her hair also showed Him more love and respect than Simon. She was forgiven her past transgressions and held up by Jesus as a beautiful example of one who truly understands the miraculous gift of mercy.

Although most of us may not identify with the specific sin of these two promiscuous women, the field is leveled as we relate to them as redeemed recipients of God's mercy and joint heirs in Christ.

The parable of the prodigal son (Luke 15:11-32) is further evidence of what mercy should look like in our lives. We know from this story that one son remains reliable and loyal to his father, while the other son dishonors their father by demanding his inheritance early, flaking on his responsibilities, and leaving home—only to squander the money on unrighteous living.

Once he finds himself destitute (to the point of slopping with pigs and desperate for a way out of his situation), he decides to return home and beg forgiveness from his father. Owning his shame and relinquishing his rights as a son, he is willing to take his place as a servant in his father's household.

However, the father, filled with joy and relief at his son's return, shows favor on him. Even though his son's rebellion had undoubtedly broken his heart and caused him great anguish, we do not hear of him punishing or chastising his son. Instead, he shows only mercy, as he restores him to the family and calls for a feast to celebrate his homecoming.

The older brother's response to his brother's return was an entirely different story. He was incensed that his foolish brother was being treated with such kindness, respect, and generosity. He perceived his father to be actually rewarding his brother for his appalling behavior by having a fattened calf killed, the best robe and ring given to him, and a feast given in his honor. He did not seem to grasp the concept of mercy, at least not where his brother was concerned.

Mercy doesn't consider what is fair. It is not based on merit. Mercy, much like grace, is based on an act of benevolence: never deserved, always welcomed by the recipient, but not always understood or embraced by those around them.

Many criminals are shown mercy: either by a judge in court, or a parole board, or ultimately, by the only One who truly pardons. I think it's fair to say though, that for most humans, there is a great need to see people get there just punishment for wrong actions—especially when it comes to inflicting pain and suffering or infringing on the rights of others.

This innate sense of justice within us comes from the very nature of God. However, God's loving nature is also one of mercy. It is sometimes hard for us to reconcile the two. We want people to be punished. Punishment represents justice. Punishment is designed to deter people from repeating their wrong behavior. Punishment brings some measure of solace to victims of crimes. It can also sometimes bring restitution—and, at times, even restoration.

But we must allow room for God's mercy. Saul of Tarsus received mercy. The thief on the cross received mercy. The woman who was not stoned received mercy. Every true believer receives mercy. Where would we be without God's mercy?

Yet although we might hate to admit it, we can sometimes resemble the unmerciful servant more than the merciful king or the hard-hearted older son rather than the forgiving father.

One day, there will no longer be a need for mercy. The just Judge will separate those who are evil from those who are found righteous by the shed blood of Jesus. Although He extended His love and forgiveness to all (John 3:16), only those who love, honor, and obey Him receive an eternal pardon. For those who have rejected Him, He will impose His mighty wrath.

While on earth, we are given many opportunities to show God's love and mercy to those around us. In those times when we find it difficult to extend mercy, we need to remember that God calls us to love others, not judge them. We can trust Him, even when things seem totally unjust. He knows all and sees all and will set things right in the end. We also need to remind ourselves just how much mercy has been shown us when so undeserved. As we do, emotions such as anger and frustration give way to a desire to see another life radically changed and restored to the Father.

1. Read John 8:1-11. Think about a specific situation in your life when God's mercy was clearly extended to you. How did it make you feel? Guilty? Grateful? Liberated? Or? (Fill in the blank):

2. Read Matthew 18:21-35. Think of a time when you withheld mercy from someone. How did you justify that decision in your mind? In what way might that decision have caused damage to that relationship? In looking back, do you believe a merciful response could have led to a better outcome?

CHAPTER 8

JOY

All my springs of joy are in you.
Psalm 87:7

In order for us to have an accurate picture of the gift of joy that God bestows on His children, it might be helpful to first examine the definition of joy, to determine whether or not it can be distinguished from the word "happiness." Many Christians believe that there is a great deal of difference between the definitions of "happiness" and "joy." They would tell you that happiness is based on external circumstances and can be very unpredictable and temporary. Whereas, joy emanates from an internal manifestation of a deep, lasting blessedness and is constant in nature.

Let's begin by looking at various definitions that have been assigned to these two words. In the online Merriam-Webster Dictionary, they appear to be interchangeable:[29]

---

[29] Randy Alcorn, *Is There a Difference Between Happiness and Joy?*, quoting *Merriam-Webster Unabridged Dictionary* (*www.epm.org*, 11-11-15).

Happiness (n): a state of well-being and contentment: JOY

Joy (n): a state of happiness or felicity: BLISS

When you look up the word "happiness" in the Baker's Evangelical Dictionary of Biblical Theology, it says: "see JOY."

And when you look up the word "Joy" in the same dictionary, its leading definition states: "Happiness over an unanticipated or present good."[30]

Aristotle, the well-known Greek philosopher, once defined happiness as "the meaning and purpose of life, the aim and end of human existence."[31]

From a biblical perspective, author Hugh Whelchel, of *The Institute for Faith, Works and Economics*, explains that the Old Testament word *"ashrê"* translates in English to mean: ' "well-being," "flourishing," and "happiness." This word is most often translated into English as "blessed." '

Further, he says: " 'Ashrê is used in passages like Psalm 1, which starts, "Blessed/Happy/Flourishing is the man..." (Psalm 1:1). 'Ashrê is used throughout the Psalms and Proverbs to describe the happy state of those who live wisely according to God's design.

This same formula for 'ashrê is used in the New Testament with the word *makarios*, the Greek equivalent of 'ashrê.'

---

[30] [33] Elwell, Walter A., editor, *Baker's Evangelical Dictionary of Biblical Theology* (1996).

[31] Greg Laurie, *God's Definition of Happiness* (www.wnd.com 5-29-10).

Thus, *ʾashrê/makarios* is making an appeal to true happiness and flourishing through obedience within the gracious covenant God has given to his people."[32]

In light of this (that the term "happiness" actually has its origins in the Bible), we can begin to make a strong case for espousing that the words "happiness" and "joy" are synonyms. However, let's probe further...

Over the years, I have counseled both believers and non-believers alike who were "unhappy" and were searching for true happiness in their lives. Having been influenced by numerous sermons and other teachings on this matter of happiness versus joy, I myself had come to believe that the two were entirely separate states of being.

I settled on the familiar notion that happiness was more of a transitory state of being, since it was dependent on fragile criteria (such as feelings, comfort zones, and other people's responses and/or behavior). Whereas, joy was rock-solid, based on faith in God "with whom there is no variation or shifting shadow" (James 1:17 NASB) and possible to experience even when in the midst of great sorrow. I felt comfortable explaining the differences—highlighting the fact that although happiness is commonly sought after and often defined in more tangible ways, it lacks substance and therefore, is elusive in nature. Joy, on the other hand, is more desirable, because it is enduring and deeply rooted in absolute truth.

Along the way, however, as my knowledge of God's Word grew and my understanding of these two terms

---

[32] Hugh Whelchel, The Biblical Definition of Happiness (The Institute for Faith, Works and Economics, www.ifwe.org, August 8, 2016).

became more well-defined, I came to realize that these two terms should not be compartmentalized.

The issue is not whether a person should be "happy" versus "joyful." The real matter at hand is whether or not pursuing earthly pleasures can bring true and lasting joy (happiness), more than seeking the things of God. That leads us to explore the concept of *pleasure*.

There is nothing wrong with pleasure. After all, God created pleasure. In fact, in Philippians 2:13 (NASB) it tells us that God's interaction with us and His purposes for us are "for *His* good pleasure" (*emphasis mine*). Further, Revelation 4:11 confirms to us "for thy pleasure they are and were created" (KJV). God takes delight in us.[33] He enjoys us. He takes pleasure in us.

God also created pleasure for humans to enjoy. He designed sexual intimacy between a husband and wife most assuredly, for the purpose of procreation, but also for their pleasure as well.[34] Psalm 37:4 tells of His promise to all believers that if we delight ourselves (take pleasure) in Him, He will give us the desires of our heart. In Psalm 16:11, He assures His faithful ones of "eternal pleasures" as well.

These passages provide evidence that not only does He derive pleasure from us, but through our knowing Him, obeying Him, and worshiping Him, we will also find our pleasure in Him.

He also clearly illustrates in Ecclesiastes 2:1-11 that chasing after earthly pleasures more than Him does not bring joy (happiness). In fact, it is meaningless (v. 11). Instead, He tells us, "Seek first his kingdom and

---

[33] Ps. 147:11; Zeph. 3:17.

[34] Prov. 5:18-19; Song of Solomon 1:16; 5:10-16.

his righteousness, and all these things will be given to you as well" (Matt. 6:33).

God wants to bless us. It brings Him great pleasure to see His children "filled with an inexpressible and glorious joy" (1 Pet. 1:8), which He promises can be experienced here and now—even in this fallen world in which we live. Yet many choose to follow the ways of the world. Many are led astray by subtle enticements that eventually lead to their own destruction[35]

Let us do a brief case study on Solomon. As a son of King David, he was given a good start in life. His childhood was not without some family drama, but overall, he had a godly father who loved him and left him a rich heritage as "a man after God's own heart" (1 Sam. 13:14).

As the torch was passed down to him, Solomon walked closely with God. In fact, so much so, that God offered him "whatever he wanted" (2 Chron. 1:7). He could have asked for all kinds of earthly treasures, but he didn't. He also could have sought after other earthly pleasures, but instead, he asked God for wisdom and knowledge.

He recognized his high honor and privilege to rule over his people. He understood how God's favor was upon him. He wanted to honor God by being a good and godly king. In turn, God rewarded him for being humble in his request, knowing it came from a pure heart.

> *Since this is your heart's desire and you*
> *have not asked for wealth, riches or honor,*
> *nor for the death of your enemies, and*

---

[35] James 1:15.

*since you have not asked for a long life but
for wisdom and knowledge to govern my
people over whom I have made you king,
therefore wisdom and knowledge will be
given you. And I will also give you wealth,
riches and honor, such as no king who was
before you ever had and none after you will
have.*

2 Chronicles 1:11-12

What a blessed reminder this passage is for all believers: that as we fully surrender our fleshly desires and agendas to Him, yielding ourselves completely to His purposes, He is exalted and we receive the blessings that come from His approval.

Because Solomon put God's agenda ahead of his own, God blessed him "exceedingly abundantly" above and beyond what he had asked for (Eph. 3:20). We can imagine from the description of his royal palace (found in 1 Kings 7) that Solomon's home must have been the epitome of a palatial mansion, especially since it took thirteen years to build. We also know that with at least 4,000 stalls for his horses and chariots and 12,000 horses, his wealth must have been widely known and greatly admired.[36]

However, wealth and admiration don't guarantee happiness. Consider, for example, the proverbial lottery winner, who suddenly finds himself obscenely rich and popular, but soon discovers that fame and fortune can never truly satisfy the deepest longings of the heart.

---

[36] 2 Chron. 9:25

Moreover, he can also find that riches and status can easily vanish as quickly as they were obtained.

In the case of Solomon, he did not need to win the lottery. He experienced something far greater—a relationship with God. However, when he turned away from God (as he began to take on foreign wives and make sacrifices to foreign gods), he fell out of favor with the God who had given him so much:

> *So Solomon did evil in the eyes of the LORD;*
> *he did not follow the LORD completely, as*
> *David his father had done. (1 Kings 11:6)*

> *The LORD became angry with Solomon*
> *because his heart had turned away from*
> *the LORD, the God of Israel. (v. 9)*

Because of his foolish choices, God removed His hand of grace from Solomon. Instead, He promised to "tear the kingdom away" from him (vv. 11-13). Here he had been given everything anyone could ever want or hope for in this life: wisdom, respect, and earthly riches beyond measure, and above all, covenantal love and great favor with God.

In the end, however, he was bankrupt of more than just his wealth. He had sold his soul for earthly pleasures and paid a high price. He lost his standing with God. He lost his stature as a wise and godly king. His son would suffer from the sins of his father by witnessing the tearing away of his kingdom (vv. 11-12).

God's Word assures us numerous times that earthly treasures and pleasures can never fulfill us like heavenly riches and rewards can. In 1 Timothy 6 we are also asked to admonish others:

> *not to put their hope in wealth, which is uncertain, but to put their hope in God, who richly provides us with everything for our enjoyment. Command them to do good, to be rich in good deeds, and to be generous and willing to share. In this way they will lay up treasure for themselves as a firm foundation for the coming age, so that they may take hold of the life that is truly life.*
> *1 Timothy 6:17-19*

The secret to being happy in this life isn't really a secret at all. It is loving God with all your heart, soul, strength, and mind. It is loving others as yourself. It is not in buying nice clothes, fast cars, large homes, or having a successful career. Sure, those things can give us pleasure, but if they become the central focus of our lives, they will never bring us true joy and they give no lifetime guarantee.

In the Northern California fires of 2017, many lost everything they had: loved ones, homes, pets, their livelihood, pictures and other precious treasures—gone forever. Some people have rebuilt their homes, while others are still rebuilding or have started all over again elsewhere. Still others are stuck in a time warp and may never be able to get past the horror of the fire and the enormity of their loss.

One couple, the daughter and son-in-law of a dear friend of mine, were among those who lost their home. Among the things most precious to them were their family pictures, a special turkey platter, an antique guitar collection, and their barn (where they had hosted many weddings over the years).

The aftermath of such a loss resulted in pain of epic proportions. Along with all the tears and sadness, they had to deal with the logistical nightmare of starting over: immediate needs, apartment living, dealing with various agencies, waiting to rebuild, working with the contractor, furnishing the rebuild without having any of their personal effects, and enduring a second evacuation two months after they occupied their newly-rebuilt home. However, due to their strong faith in God, they were able to testify to God's faithfulness, and the enduring joy walking with Him brings—even in the midst of suffering.

Likewise, a precious friend whom I have known for many years is the embodiment of a joy-filled Christian who truly praises God in all circumstances. She has valiantly battled cancer for some time now, and recently learned that she is terminal. Yet she always maintains her outward joy through an inner peace and assurance that God will be with her, He will sustain her, and she can look forward to an eternal future with a new glorified body, free of pain and suffering.

One of the best definitions I have come across to describe true joy comes from author and speaker Kay Warren: "Joy is the settled assurance that God is in control of all the details of my life, the quiet confidence that ultimately everything is going to be alright, and the determined choice to praise God in all things."[37]

---

[37] Rick Warren, *Transformed: How God Changes Us Study Guide* (Saddleback Church, 2014), p. 204.

Famous Bible scholar, Oswald Chambers (1874-1917) claimed that, "There is no mention in the Bible of happiness for a Christian."[38] Likewise, it's common to hear people make claims like this, "Joy is in 155 verses in the KJV Bible, happiness isn't in the Bible." [39] However, the truth of the matter is that the word "happy" is found in the King James translation numerous times (see Job 5:17; Prov. 3:13; John 13:17).

So now that we've established a reasonable basis for defining joy and happiness as being one and the same, let's look at some other aspects about joy. Famous pastor/evangelist/author, Greg Laurie observes:

> So religious or spiritual people tend to be happier people. But I would take it a step further and add that godly people are happy people. According to the Bible, if we seek to know God and discover His plan for our lives, we will find the happiness that has eluded us for so long. In other words, happiness does not come from seeking *it*, but from seeking *Him*, because "Happy are the people whose God is the Lord!" (Ps. 144:15 NKJV). God built us to turn to Him and find our fulfillment, our contentment and our happiness in a relationship with him.[40]

---

[38] Randy Alcorn, *Is There a Difference Between Happiness and Joy?* (www.epm.org 11-11-15).

[39] *Ibid.*, quoting *"In Your Opinion, What's the Difference between Joy and Happiness?* Yahoo Answers

[40] Greg Laurie, *God's Definition of Happiness* (www. wnd.com 5-29-10).

Yet this notion of true joy or happiness has to be qualified to some degree. John MacArthur, in his *New Testament Commentary on Galatians* writes: 'The faithful, effective Christian life, however, is not simply a great emotional adventure filled with wonderful feelings and experiences. It is first of all the humble pursuit of God's truth and will and of conformity to it. The obedient Christian experiences joy and satisfaction beyond measure, far exceeding that of superficial believers who constantly seek spiritual "highs." Life in Christ is not sterile and joyless. But true joy (happiness), satisfaction, and all other such feelings are by-products of knowing and obeying God's truth.'[41]

Another real issue confronting and often confounding many believers is in regards to the notion that we are to have joy in the midst of our trials and suffering. It is not a matter of whether we are able to have joy. It is more a matter of do we choose to have joy—no matter how difficult or painful our situation. James tells us to "consider it pure joy...whenever you face trials of many kinds" (James 1:2). How exactly is this possible?

The answer is found in God's steadfast and sacrificial love for us. It is found in His grace and great mercy for us. It is found in His trustworthy promises and eternal hope given to us.

In Nehemiah chapter 8, Nehemiah attests to the fact that "the joy of the Lord is [our] strength" (v. 10). At the time these words were coined, the wall had just been rebuilt. The exiles had been brought back to Jerusalem

---

[41] John MacArthur, *The MacArthur New Testament Commentary on Galatians* (The Moody Bible Institute, 1987), p. 64.

and gathered at the town square to hear Ezra read from the Book of the Law of Moses. As he read, they wept and mourned bitterly for they had come under deep conviction of their past sins, of their disobedience that had splintered their people and had taken them into captivity. Yet Ezra instructs them: "Do not mourn or weep" (v. 9). "Go and enjoy choice food and sweet drinks...This day is sacred to our Lord. Do not grieve" (v. 10).

When we go through times of hardship, persecution, or grief, it is easy to fully immerse ourselves in the deep pain and emotions we feel. We must by no means suppress our pain and emotions, but *we must not also be ruled by them.* The beauty of Nehemiah's admonishment to his people is that it serves to remind us, as it did them, that God both desires to and is able to bring beauty from ashes (Isa. 61:3) and joy after the dark night of grief (Ps. 30:5).

Through our suffering, we can identify with Him in both death and in resurrection life (Phil. 3:10). As we endure painful trials, we become more like Him,[42] which pleases Him and results in our being a fragrant aroma that attracts others to Him (2 Cor. 15-16). He assures us that as we surrender to His will, no matter how hard, no matter the hurting, He will bring forth good for us and ultimate glory to himself.

Is it hard to be joyful in hard times? Yes, of course, it certainly can be—especially when it's not been a habitual choice. As we lean into Jesus more and more, and lean on God's promises, we will experience both His joy and His peace beyond our understanding.

---

[42] Rom. 5:3-5; 1 Pet. 1:3-7.

How completely humbling to have in the Trinity—this amazing trio of: "the God of all comfort" (2 Cor. 1:3); Jesus our closest friend; and the Holy Spirit our Helper. In them, we are given all the resources we need to joyfully endure the difficulties we face in this life.

Paul gives us a reassuring testimony of what it looks like to have joy in the midst of adversity. When he was attacked by a mob, unjustly arrested, severely beaten, then imprisoned, his attitude and actions were consistent with the call to joy we are all to have.[43] In verse 25 of Acts 16, even though he is physically in agony and being prevented from preaching the gospel, we find him "praying and singing hymns to God." He is not throwing himself a pity party. He is not focusing on his physical pain. He is praising God! And, as he worships along with Silas, he is exemplifying a strong witness to others. When the earthquake hits and he and Silas have a chance to escape, he shows his integrity and displays compassion for the jailer when he reassures the jailer that they have not fled. How effective a witness is a joy-filled, godly response!

When our internal joy manifests itself on the outside, it opens doors untold to further the kingdom. One key factor in Paul maintaining his joy is that he never forgot the source of his joy. He clung to the Vine (John 15:5). He never forgot that he was an unworthy sinner whom God loved enough to send His Son to die in his place. He remembered that God was always with him—no matter his hardships. And finally, he remembered that he had a blessed eternity awaiting him.

---

[43] Acts 16:19-23.

We are told in 1 Thessalonians 5:16 to "Be joyful always." When Jesus told His disciples that He would be leaving them, He assured them that, "Now is your time of grief, but...no one will take away your joy" (John 16:22). True joy in the Lord can never be taken from us. We have been given so many reasons to be full of joy. As we daily abide in the Vine—spending quality time with Him, meditating on His Word as we go about our day, and watching His blessings continue to unfold before us, we are sure to experience the perpetual joy that the psalmist proclaims in Psalm 126, "The Lord has done great things for us, and we are filled with joy" (v. 3).

1. Read Psalm 126:3. How does exemplifying a joyful spirit reflect the Spirit-filled life? Look up Job 9:27 and Proverbs 17:22. What benefits are there to being consistently joyful, rather than chronically sad?

2. Read 1 Thessalonians 5:16. Does this verse imply that we are never to feel sadness? How do you reconcile this verse with passages such as Ecclesiastes 1:18 and John 11:35?

3. Read James 1:2. How can we experience joy in the midst of our trials? Cite two of God's promises that are helpful to hold onto when enduring a difficult trial.

CHAPTER 9

PEACE

You will keep in perfect peace him whose
mind is steadfast, because he trusts in you.
Isaiah 26:3

A number of songs have been written and sung about
peace over the years. Heartfelt words, expressing
hope for peace among all people and that the majority
of the world longs to see come to pass. Sadly, however, the world has been riddled with wars, unrest,
and violence for centuries. Still, God has called each
of us to be peacemakers and has also offered the gift
of peace to anyone who receives His gift of salvation,
from the very beginning of time. And His gift is two-
fold: (1) Forever peace one day, when there will be no
more sadness, pain, or tears; and (2) perfect peace
right now, as people of faith place their complete trust
and hope in Him.

These are such beautiful promises for believers—
promises that sustain us through the difficult times we
face, whether losing a loved one, losing a job, or losing
hope in some other way. It is a tremendous future

blessing for people of faith to look forward to peace in our eternal state someday. Unfortunately, though, many Christians put all their focus on their heavenly inheritance and forget that they can enjoy the blessing of God's perfect peace while still living in this earthly existence.

I remember when our beloved pastor passed away at only forty-three years of age. It was such a shock to everyone. There was grief all around me. Now I'm not saying that I didn't feel any grief at all. Even today, I still miss this humble, godly man and the profound influence he had on helping me become a true disciple. However, I felt God's protection and peace in a very special way during that initial time of grieving. It was that "peace that passes all understanding" that is promised to us in Philippians 4:7 when we draw near to Him.

When I went to the funeral home for the viewing, I just looked at him and saw this empty shell of a man. I didn't cry. Certainly, I felt sadness at this loss—more so for the beautiful family he left behind, than anything else—but I could clearly see that his spirit was gone. He was at peace with the Lord. I would see him again one day.

To some degree, I even felt joy in that moment, as I reflected on his strong testimony—how many lives he impacted in his short life and all that he had taught me. It is spiritual truths like these, that are hard for an unbeliever to grasp, yet comforting to a believer, and important for a believer to reflect to others. Resting on God's strength, my peaceful heart and countenance enabled me to comfort others who were overcome by grief.

Believers may sometimes forget that "as far as it depends on [us], [we are to] live at peace with everyone"

(Rom. 12:18). God expects believers to spread His message of hope and true peace. To do so, however, we have to bear it out authentically in our own lives. God gives us ample opportunities to transition His truths from "head knowledge" to "heart knowledge." Knowing what God's Word says is one thing, but to really appropriate truth where it counts, is where the rubber meets the road. Just imagine what the world would be like if every believer was fully faithful and obedient to everything God commanded—this is the challenge set before the Body of Christ—and it starts with each one of us.

We live in a world where many have a "me first" mentality. It's why there is so much abuse—and the reason why the divorce rate is so high—and it's often how wars begin. Asserting our rights out of selfishness, when it hurts or deprives someone else, is not consistent with what the Bible teaches or what Jesus modeled so perfectly. Humility is key in perpetuating peace. Romans 8:6 tells us that "the mind set on the flesh is death, but the mind controlled by the Spirit is life and peace." We must walk in the Spirit continually if we want to experientially know peace and contribute to bringing peace and order to the world around us.

Unfortunately, because we live in a fallen world, conflicts and confrontations are inevitable. Whether a sinner or a sinner saved by grace, we all will rub up against people who do not share our same views, values, or priorities. When conflicts arise, the best starting point for bringing resolution is to pray for our attitude to be right before the Lord and to pray for the other person or other parties involved. Confrontation is never usually an easy or comfortable task. Whether you are the one confronting or the one being confronted, someone is being hit with negative feedback that can be very hurtful—even resulting in long-term damage to the individual or to the relationship, especially if not approached with a loving attitude.

There is an old adage that says, "There are those who love to speak the truth, and those who speak the truth in love." God never wants us to be gleeful about pointing out someone else's flaws or failures. In fact, He says in Matthew 7:3, "Why do you look at the speck of sawdust in your brother's eye and pay no attention to the plank in your own eye?" We must seek to sow seeds of peace. And when confrontation is necessary, we must pray up ahead and do it with an attitude of love and humility.

It must break God's heart when He sees His beloved creation at odds with one another. From early on in human history, there has been strife. Cain killed his brother Abel, Jacob betrayed Esau, Joseph was sold into slavery by his brothers, Saul was jealous of David, and the list goes on. However, God makes it clear to us that we have been given "the ministry of reconciliation" (2 Cor. 5:18). We see a beautiful example of what this ministry should look like for us, in stories such as in the book of Hosea, as well as in the parable of the prodigal son (Luke 15:11-32).

As we draw ever-nearer to the conclusion of this earth age, we are witnessing the increase of evil, as many people are becoming more and more "lovers of themselves, lovers of money, boastful, proud, abusive... without love...brutal, not lovers of the good...lovers of pleasure rather than lovers of God—having a form of godliness but denying its power" (2 Tim. 3:2-5). Now, more than ever, we need to be actively pursuing this ministry to reconcile with others and most importantly, to direct them to the reconciliation God offers to all.

St. Francis of Assisi (1181/2-1226) long ago wrote an iconic prayer that encapsulates this ministry of reconciliation we have been given:

> *Lord, make me a channel of your peace;*
> *where there is hatred, let me sow love;*
> *where there is injury, pardon;*
> *where there is doubt, faith;*
> *where there is despair, hope;*
> *where there is darkness, light;*
> *where there is sadness, joy.*
>
> *O, divine Master, grant that I may not*
> *so much seek to be understood, as to*
> *understand; to be loved, as to love;*
> *For it is in giving that we receive,*
> *it is in pardoning that we are pardoned;*
> *and it is in dying that we are born to*
> *eternal life. Amen.*[44]

World peace is a lofty goal. It starts with us being the change we want to see in our own sphere of influence. It is in our modeling Christ's humble nature that we can begin to see the world become more of what it should be—even if it will never be entirely what we would want it to be: a world where love, mercy, generosity, kindness, patience, peace, and forgiveness reign triumphant.

---

[44]

1. According to Romans 8:6, what does "the mind set on the flesh" lead to? What does this verse tell us about setting our mind on the Spirit?

2. Look up Proverbs 14:30, Philippians 4:6-7, and James 1:6-8. What are some of the barriers we create that prevent us from experiencing God's perfect peace?

CHAPTER 10

WISDOM

If any of you lacks wisdom, he should ask
God, who gives generously to all without
finding fault, and it will be given to you.

James 1:5

Godly wisdom is ours for the asking, but it is not something that we automatically possess when we become saved. According to Proverbs 3:13-15, wisdom is something to be desired, sought, and acquired.

On a daily basis, we are faced with many decisions. Some decisions affect only us, but others will affect people around us as well. As we search the Scriptures, we can see how wisdom blesses those who walk in it, and often those who are secondary beneficiaries of it. We can also see how a lack of wisdom can bring shame upon a person, a family, a country, or an entire people. It can bring devastating consequences—including death and destruction.

King David is arguably the greatest biblical example of someone who walked in wisdom. This, despite the fact that the Bible tells us that his son, Solomon, held that prestigious place of honor in history, as he possessed extraordinary wisdom (1 Kings 3:13)—at least, that is, until his downfall of turning away from God. Wisdom, once obtained, is usually not lost, but in the case of King Solomon, tragically, it was.

Early on in his reign as king, Solomon, for the most part, walked in obedience to the Lord—with the exception that "he offered sacrifices and burned incense on the high places." (1 Kings 3:3). Because Solomon walked with God, God offered to give him anything he wanted and was pleased to honor his request for wisdom.

Not only did God make him wiser, but he also made him more wise than any other alive—then, now, or ever (v. 12). Wow! What a gift to be given! Can you imagine what it would be like to be that wise? Even though none of us will ever possess wisdom to the degree Solomon did, seeking and receiving God's wisdom by any measure is one of the greatest benefits any of us could ever receive as true believers.

Believers often highlight many virtues and blessings of the Christian life: faith, hope, love, joy, peace, grace, mercy, and forgiveness. Yet it seems to me that wisdom, though invaluable, seems not to be quite as widely emphasized as the others.

Proverbs is full of verses that extol the virtues of wisdom. In chapter 4:6, we are promised that wisdom "will protect you." In verse 7 of same chapter, we learn that "wisdom is supreme," and in verse 8, that if we "esteem her and embrace her, she will exalt and honor [us]." Further, in chapter 16, verse16, we discover that wisdom is even better than gold. And finally, in Proverbs 19:8, we are told we "will soon prosper" when we "cherish understanding"—understanding being directly linked to wisdom.

All this certainly held true in Solomon's case—at least as long as he walked in faithful obedience to God. Not only was he able to resolve difficult situations (such as the case of mom v. mom—1 Kings 3:16-28), but in so doing, he won the respect of the people and he also prospered greatly (1 Kings 10:23-29). However, once he began to compromise his faith, turning aside from God by taking on many wives and worshiping other gods (1 Kings 11), his wisdom was lost—much like Samson losing his Herculean strength and his favor with God, once he revealed to Delilah the source of his strength (Judges 16).

Down through the ages, God's gift of wisdom, when correctly applied in times of decision-making (whether a personal decision or one that impacts a number of people), has had far-reaching effects by providing solutions, quelling arguments, diffusing danger and has even prevented wars from starting in many cases.

King David knew this principle well as he ruled over Israel. Nine times, we read throughout his reign that, "David inquired of the LORD" at very pivotal moments.[45] What a simple, yet effective pattern of fearing the Lord and seeking after His will David has set before us. If only we followed this pattern at every turn, every decision, at every moment of doubt, fear, or worry.

As we are assured in James 1:5, God stands ready to dispense wisdom generously to those who ask him. If we don't receive it, it is either because we have not bothered to ask Him for it or there is some sin barrier

---

[45] See 1 Sam.23:2-3, 4-5,10-11, 12-14; 2 Sam. 2:1; 5:17-21, 22-25; 21:1.

causing blockage so that He cannot answer, much less, hear our request.[46] Pride is the primary culprit when we don't pray for wisdom as we should (Prov. 3:7, 11:2). Pride causes us to speak before we seek (13:3), be quick to anger (14:29), and resist godly counsel and discipline (19:20).

Proverbs, one of three "wisdom books" in the Bible (along with Ecclesiastes and Job), offers us multiple ways to obtain wisdom and keep it: by fearing Him (9:10), praying for wisdom (2:1-6), and by manifesting the qualities God expects of us—to be humble (11:2), patient, peace-loving, considerate, submissive, full of mercy and good fruit, impartial, and sincere (3:17).

In Matthew 7:24, we are also asked to put these things into practice, so that we will stand secure on solid ground. As we submit to God in all these areas, we are well poised to receive the wisdom that we are lacking.

Wisdom is most often associated with decision-making. The outcome of a decision is dictated by how wise or unwise was the basis for the decision.

For example, in the case of Moses, he began his mission for God by deciding to doubt God, rather than trust Him when first given the assignment to lead his people out of Egypt. Had he continued to walk in fear, he would have missed out on all the blessings he received, including the honor of delivering his people from the bondage of slavery (Exod. 4).

As he obeyed God in each step of his mission, he came to know God's character better and better: His faithfulness, justice, righteousness, love, compassion,

---

[46] Isa. 59:2

and His mercy. Knowing that God was right there with him, helping him as he faced tremendous challenges, enabled him to grow more confident and to make even wiser decisions along the way.

Of course, just like with us, it was quite the learning process. When Moses returned to Egypt to confront Pharaoh, the people turned on Moses for causing them more hardship (Exod. 5:6-21). Once again, we find him doubting God, "O Lord, why have you brought trouble upon this people? Is this why you sent me? Ever since I went to Pharaoh to speak in your name, he has brought trouble upon this people, and you have not rescued your people at all" (vv. 22-23).

Over time, however, as God took Moses to deeper levels of understanding of His love for him and His people, it became easier to trust Him. As his level of trust grew, God was able to use him in mighty ways—inciting the plagues, coordinating the mass exodus out of Egypt, leading his people through the Red Sea while being chased by Pharaoh's army, defeating the Amalekites and more.

The wisdom that he gained, as he incrementally trusted God more and more, not only brought blessing upon blessing on his own life, but it also paid great dividends for an entire nation. The majority of decisions Moses made had a direct impact on all those for whom he was responsible. It should serve as a constant reminder for us, as we face important decisions in our lives, that those decisions can also have a profound effect on those around us.

We may never have to carry the enormous weight on our shoulders for others as Moses did as he led his people out of Egypt, or when he led them through their long, protracted wilderness wanderings, or served as the first judge of his people. However, we should never take lightly that the decisions we do make have the potential to positively or negatively affect others' lives.

Proverbs 9:10 tells us: "The fear of the LORD is the beginning of wisdom." David could make his inquiries to the Lord and believe he would hear from Him with confidence because he faithfully submitted himself to Him with a humble, penitent, and grateful heart. He spent countless hours daily in prayer, worship, and praise—this should be our top priority every day as well.

Surrounding ourselves with godly people is another way we acquire wisdom (see Prov. 13:20). This doesn't mean that we never associate with unbelievers or with friends who are not as far along in their Christian faith as us. However, it does mean that we are assured to "grow in wisdom and stature" (Luke 2:52), as we place ourselves consistently among some mature believers who will enhance our knowledge and understanding on spiritual matters.

When we find ourselves in a difficult situation, seeking wise counsel from a mature believer (one who can objectively assess the situation and perhaps share from their own life experience) helps in giving us a clearer perspective.

Pastor's sermons, Bible studies, apps, videos, books, and many other resources can also be great influencers and benefit our growth in wisdom tremendously. Of course, we have to be on our guard. We need to scrutinize carefully what teachings and influences we allow into our lives, as we can easily be led astray if we don't hold them up against the lens of Scripture.

As mentioned earlier, Proverbs 3:15 strongly recommends that we should seek out and highly value wisdom as "nothing [we] desire can compare with her." The path of wisdom always leads us to a deeper understanding of God's nature, His will, and His ways.

1. Read Proverbs 23:23. How do we acquire wisdom, discipline and understanding (see Ps. 111:10, Jas. 1:5, and Jas. 3:13)?

2. Read Proverbs 11:2. How does pride prevent us from acquiring wisdom?

3. In what ways can a lack of wisdom be harmful? In what ways can acquiring wisdom be helpful?

CHAPTER 11

RESTORATION

He restores my soul.

Psalm 23:3

God is in the restoration business. Even as Adam and Eve made the choice to disobey God in the Garden of Eden, bringing about immediate and life-changing separation in their relationship with God, He had already made a long-range provision to restore them and the rest of humankind back to Himself.

Next, fast forward to Noah. When God saw how corrupt humans had become, He knew He had to destroy almost the entire human race in order to eradicate the evil that had taken root and spread like an aggressive cancer. Yet He chose to save a remnant that would be a crucial link to the hope for redemption in generations to come.

After the flood, however, it did not take long for the prideful nature of man to once again resurface and toss aside the godly statutes and precepts God had set in place, as people desired to become gods of their own making. Those presumptuous builders of the Tower of

Babel could not succeed, just as no one who attempts to reach heaven by their own merit or tries to equal the one true God can ever succeed.

Time and again throughout the course of human history, we have seen a pattern of humans seeking to subvert God's authority and strike out on their own. Yet God in His infinite mercy continues to display great patience, while offering forgiveness to those willing to yield to His authority in their lives.

The story of the late Louis Zamperini (1917-2014)[47] is a classic example of God's restoration. He was someone who although early on was determined to live life on his own terms, eventually surrendered to God and went on to be used mightily for kingdom service (but not without first suffering devastating consequences from his stubborn, willful choices). While he was still a rebellious young man in his teen years, he discovered running as a way to release some of his angst. His drive, coupled with his natural athleticism, soon earned him a spot on the Olympic team. He was well on his way to a promising running career.

However, when the war broke out, he decided to enlist and was a pilot in the Army Air Corps. After his plane was shot down, he fought to stay alive and, by God's grace, miraculously survived forty-seven days out at sea. It was during this desperate period, when he didn't know whether he would live or die, that he tried to bargain with God. He made a promise that if God would allow him to survive, he would serve Him for the rest of his life. God did spare his life, and even though he had to endure being beaten and tortured while a

---

[47] *Unbroken* film (Universal Pictures, 2014).

prisoner of war, he was eventually able to return home to the States. Upon his return (and for a number of years afterwards), he forgot the promise he had made to God—living only for his own pleasure.

It took the threat of losing his family and subsequently attending a Billy Graham Crusade to get his attention and remind him of the commitment he had once made to God. Even though he had drifted far from God, God did not give up on him. He did a one-eighty, and went on to share his powerful testimony with many people—becoming good friends with Billy Graham and speaking at some of Graham's crusades.

When people are broken, God longs to heal them. In fact, He *can* and *does* heal them. They need only to believe that He can, just like the bleeding woman did in Mark 5:25-34. When people are directionless and searching for meaning for their lives (as was the case of the sinful woman in John 4), God's Holy Spirit refreshes and renews them with Living Water. When people are delivered from their greatest fears (as the disciples were after the resurrection—John 20), God brings renewed hope, confidence, even boldness. When people are resentful or hateful (as was Paul in Act 8:1, when persecuting Jews), God can replace their heart of stone with a heart of flesh (Acts 9:10), as they acknowledge His lordship in their lives.

God has a long history of saving, healing, and restoring people to Himself. Even though healing and restoring can go hand in hand at times, they are not one and the same thing (more on healing in the next chapter).

He has given much, so that we might receive far more than we could ever deserve. Paul understood this principle, as he penned these words from 2 Corinthians 5:20-21, "We are therefore Christ's ambassadors, as though God were making his appeal through us. We implore you on Christ's behalf: *Be reconciled to God.* God made him who had no sin to be sin for us, so that in him we might become the righteousness of God" (*emphasis mine*).

Not only do we need to grasp the gravity of what Christ did on the cross for us and embrace this remarkable love that restores us to a right relationship with God, but we are then also given the ministry of reconciliation whereby we can encourage others to be restored to Him.

How do we go about this awesome task? When we allow ourselves to become burdened for others (wanting them to also receive pardon from sin and the freedom from guilt that we have received), we can more readily convey to others how "God was pleased to have all his fullness dwell in him, and through him to reconcile to himself all things...by making peace through his blood, shed on the cross" (Col. 1:20). Marinate on that nugget for a moment: God "*was pleased*"—despite the extreme sacrifice the Father made through His Son for each and every one of us (*emphasis mine*).

As we take up this ministry to which all believers are called, we must always keep in mind that it is not our job to save people. It is only as hearts are convicted by the Holy Spirit that their only hope is through the redeeming blood of Jesus, that they can be saved. However, He does give us the extraordinary privilege of praying for others, and along with that, testifying to His extravagant and life-giving love for them.

As we witness to others, it really is not so hard to consider sharing what God has done for us, when we think about what we were saved from (God's wrath) and what we were saved to (reconciliation with Him):

> *Since we have now been justified by his blood, how much more shall we be saved from God's wrath through him! For if, when we were God's enemies, we were reconciled to him through the death of his Son, how much more, having been reconciled, shall we be saved through his life! Not only is this so, but we also rejoice in God through our Lord Jesus Christ, through whom we have now received reconciliation.*
>
> *Romans 5:9-11*

God made a provision for all (2 Pet. 3:9b), but sadly, many will refuse His gracious offer to be restored to Him and to be partakers in a rich heavenly inheritance. For those who are reconciled to God, their lives become a glorious stream, flowing freely outward with Living Water from the Giver of Life Himself.

1. Read 2 Corinthians 5:19-6:1 and Ephesians 4:11- 13. How significant a role do believers individually play in God's restoration plan for man? What role does the Body of Christ corporately play in His plan?

2. How does the knowledge that God chooses to
   include you in His redemptive plan for humankind
   affect your sense of worth and purpose in your life
   (see 2 Cor. 6:1)?

CHAPTER 12

HEALING

For I am the LORD, who heals you.

Exodus 15:26

There is a vast sum of people in need of healing in this world—physical healing, emotional healing, and healing from mental issues. At the crux of it all, no matter the wound, damage, or defect, people are in need of spiritual healing.

God generously supplies us with encouragement in His Word as He reveals that the secret to health and our overall well-being is in putting our hope and trust in the Lord.[48] Yet many people suffer at the hands of others—they may be victims of crime, abuse, or harassment. Others suffer from self-inflicted injuries—doubt, dependency, or discontentment. Still others endure great physical pain and limitations that oftentimes interfere with their living life to the fullest.

However, despite how difficult or painful the situation, God has promised that we are "more than

---

[48] Ps. 103:2-3; Prov. 10:27; James 5:15.

conquerors through him who loved us" (Rom. 8:37). No matter what our heartaches or challenges may be, He wants us to have abundant life, and He has given us certain strategies for facing our difficulties head-on with courage and aided by the strength and comfort He offers.

Faith and Prayer

The prayer offered in faith will make the sick person well.

James 5:15

Faith and prayer go hand in hand, for "without faith, it is impossible to please God."[49] James 1:6-8 cautions us that no one who doubts will receive what they ask for because they are "unstable." However, in chapter 5 verse 16, James assures us that, "the prayer of a righteous man is powerful and effective." He goes on in verses 17-18 to remind us of Elijah—"a man just like us" whose faith-filled prayers directed the skies to withhold rain and then also pour down rain as needed.

When some prayers go unanswered, especially the kind that many people pray concerning health issues and the prolonging of life (either for themselves or for loved ones), it may seem unconscionable that God would refuse to answer a prayer of this nature. However, as mentioned previously, God is not arbitrary. He is not unjust, and He does not, on a whim, determine which prayers will be answered. He is a God of love, a God of justice, and a God of order. He always responds to

---

[49] Heb. 11:6

prayers with the intent to bring glory to His holy and magnificent name.

People seeking the Lord when in any kind of pain or anguish believe that God can bring strength, comfort, some form of relief—even complete healing to their lives. They may cry out like the psalmist in Psalm 30:2, "O LORD my God, I called to you for help and you healed me." Prayers such as this, when asking from a sincere and humble heart, can bring about miraculous healing. At times, though, God may not heal the person in the way that they might be expecting. However, God always responds to them with the intent to grow their faith (or the faith of those around them) and to shine forth His glory.

When Lazarus fell ill (John 11), his sisters Mary and Martha sent word to Jesus about their brother's failing health. They believed Jesus would quickly respond to their plea for help because they knew that Jesus had the ability to heal and because they also knew how much Jesus loved Lazarus.

In a plot twist, Jesus deliberately delayed his return to Bethany. During this time, Lazarus died and lay in his tomb for four full days. On the fourth day, Jesus returned to face a crowd—as well as a very distressed Martha, who cried out, "Lord,"..."if you had been here, my brother would not have died" (v. 21). In just a few short days, her faith experienced a severe testing.

It would be easy to try to psychoanalyze her emotions. Over the time she waited for Jesus to respond, she may have felt a mixture of fear, doubt, anger, confusion, and desperation. Many who are in the early stages of losing a loved one, struggle with denial. In her case, because of her faith, however, she may have been simply trying to remain hopeful that Jesus would still intervene as she says to him, "But I know that even now God will give you whatever you ask" (v. 22).

After Jesus tells her that Lazarus will rise again, she answers, "I know he will rise again in the resurrection at the last day" (v.24). She was not in denial. Nor was she outright delusional, as some might have thought. She was merely expressing what she believed to be true from what Jesus had taught. It was at this time, however, that she comes to a fuller realization that Jesus was not only Teacher (or "Rabbi"), but that he was "the Christ, the Son of God" (v. 27).

As the story unfolds, we can imagine that Martha and Mary were over the moon to have their brother brought back to them. It was unquestionably a miraculous physical healing. The greater point to that day, however, was the revelation of the powerful healing that Jesus brings to souls, as He is the only One who gives eternal hope to all who would believe in Him.

Jesus did, in fact, heal many physical infirmities during his earthly ministry. Although it must have given Him much joy to relieve people of their physical suffering, He always had a much greater purpose in mind: to shine the light of God's glory and reveal His merciful plan for man. His miracles came as people displayed faith (Matt. 9:1-8, 20-21); they often served to increase their faith (Matt. 15:32-39; John 11:1-40); and sometimes they served to reveal a lack of faith (Matt. 14:22-33, 17:14-20).

Humans are in desperate need of reassurance. Our fleshly nature always gravitates toward stressing and obsessing over things that are not in our power to control. The old adage, "Why pray when you can worry?"

tends to be the mindset for many a weak and weary soul. Yet there is a far better way to live.

It has been proven time and again by medical professionals that worry and stress can actually shorten a person's life. When we give our concerns over to Him, rather than fretting about them, we can actually increase the quality of our life (Prov. 14:30a). God intends for us to experience His life-giving peace and wholeness as we put our faith in Him alone.

1. Look up Exodus 15:26, Matt. 21:22, and James 5:15. How can we reconcile these verses with the reality of a situation when we (and others) prayed for healing for someone, and yet they still passed away?

2. Think of two promises from God's Word that can be shared with someone who lives with chronic pain and who is in need of hope?

CHAPTER 13

TRANSFORMATION

*Do not conform any longer to the pattern
of this world, but be transformed by the
renewing of your mind.*

Romans 12:2

Although the matter of transformation could just as easily belong under "Our Part" in part 4, it is actually God's Holy Spirit that does the bulk of the transformative work in our lives. It's true that our part is to yield, trust, follow, and obey. However, it is the Holy Spirit who prompts and guides us, gives correction, provides wisdom, and brings conviction to our hearts and minds.

So, how exactly are we transformed? The Holy Spirit is always working to mold us and bring us into alignment with God's will for our lives. He can't do all of it for us, but when we cooperate with Him by having a teachable attitude and a willing heart, He can accomplish much in us and through us.

Although the disciples had not yet received the Holy Spirit when Jesus was still with them, they had been walking very closely with Jesus and grew tremendously in their faith until the time of His death and resurrection. Once Pentecost came (Acts 2), they were indwelt with the Spirit and were able to understand and do even more for the kingdom because of that incredible gift.

As believers, we too, receive the gift of the Holy Spirit when we are born again. By His grace, we also come to know the resurrection power of Jesus. Additionally, we now have the Word of God in its entirety, along with the testimonies of many giants of the faith, such as George Muller, Charles Spurgeon, Oswald Chambers, and Billy Graham—just to name a few.

When we allow the Holy Spirit to direct our lives, we find we can deal far better with whatever comes our way. Romans 8:6 makes clear to us, "The mind of sinful man is death, but the mind controlled by the spirit is life and peace." The key phrase here is "controlled by the Spirit." Do we always let the Spirit control us? Do we "keep in step with the Spirit" every moment of every day?[50]

Transformation is an ongoing, daily, step-by-step process of *surrendering our will* so that the Holy Spirit can do His work in us. Although at the first moment of belief we became a new creation in Christ[51] (and were instantly, positionally seen as righteous in His eyes through the shed blood of Jesus), we are still being sanctified inwardly, as He renews us day by day (2 Cor. 4:16). We must die daily to our old ways (Luke 9:23), "be made new in the attitude of [our] minds" and "put on the new self" (see Eph. 4:22-24).

---

[50] Gal. 5:25

[51] 2 Cor. 5:17.

This process involves drawing nearer to God by continually *being present in His presence* through worship, praise, prayer, and by taking in His Word through Bible study, memorization, and meditation. It may sound like a lot to do, but as we put these spiritual disciplines into practice, they become as natural as breathing in and out. As we know Him and love Him more deeply, surrendering to and serving Him more faithfully, we will resemble Him more closely.

We are told in Matthew 5:48, "Be perfect...as your heavenly Father is perfect." We also find in 1 Peter 1:15, that we are commanded to "Be holy, because I am holy"—tall orders for such feeble-minded, sin-filled humans as we are! As we read verses like these, we can take heart in knowing that His plan is to not leave us in a miserable, wretched condition. In fact, He has provided all that is needed for us to become more like Him. Of course, this side of heaven, we will never be fully perfect or holy. However, that does not mean that we should give up and say, "Well, since I'm redeemed now and headed for glory, I'll just kick back and enjoy the ride." No, it's not quite that simple.

His holiness demands that we prepare for eternity *now* by our allowing Him to incrementally transform us into His likeness. Even Paul, who made such an instantaneous and radical departure from his former way of life, continued to be changed every day as he embraced his faith, endured hardships, experienced freedom, encouraged others, and sought to finish strong the race that was set before him.[52]

---

[52] Phil. 3:12-14; 2 Tim. 4:7-8.

We are also running a race—a race that requires much endurance, patience, and diligence. It also requires discipline and humility. We can't get to the finish line on our own. We are completely dependent on the Holy Spirit to guide us and spur us on. However, the hardships, the pain, and the sacrifices along the way are every bit worth the effort.

As we run our race, we can benefit greatly from becoming well-acquainted with the struggles of fellow believers, such as David and Paul (and their response to them). In Psalm 51, we see David's humility as he anguishes over his sinful state and pours out his heart before the Lord:

> *Have mercy on me, O God, according to your unfailing love; according to your great compassion blot out my transgressions. Wash away all my iniquity and cleanse me from my sin. For I know my transgressions, and my sin is always before me...Create in me a pure heart, O God, and renew a steadfast spirit within me. (vv. 1-3, 10)*

In Romans chapter 7, we see the earnestness and honesty with which Paul expresses the struggles he faces regarding his flawed condition:

> *I know that nothing good lives in me, that is, in my sinful nature. For I have the desire to do what is good, but I cannot carry it out. For what I do is not the good I want to do; no, the evil I do not want to do—this I keep on doing. Now if I do what I do not want to*

do, it is no longer I who do it, but it is sin living in me that does it.

Romans 7:18-20

Boy, can I sure relate to them! These two great men of God were sinners saved by grace, struggling with their frail, flawed humanness, longing to be transformed into the character of God—just like me. Yet, at the same time, it would be a mistake for me to compare myself with them. We each are running our own race. We must train hard for it with our eye on the prize (1 Cor. 9:24-25) and we must run our race with endurance. A great encouragement to us in this quest can be found in Hebrews 12:1-3:

> *Therefore since we are surrounded by such a great cloud of witnesses, let us throw off everything that hinders and the sin that so easily entangles, and let us run with perseverance the race marked out for us. Let us fix our eyes on Jesus, the author and perfecter of our faith, who for the joy set before him endured the cross, scorning its shame...Consider him who endured such opposition from sinful men, so that you will not grow weary and lose heart.*
>
> *Hebrews 12:1-3*

God uses various people, circumstances, and even our own weaknesses, to bring us into complete conformity to Him as He molds us into His likeness.

I had a bit of a bumpy road coming to know the Lord. God used a difficult family situation to bring me to my knees before the cross of Christ. Since then, He has continued to use challenges in my life to grow my dependence on Him and my reverence for Him.

Although, quite frankly, at times it wasn't necessarily that He was allowing me to go through challenges, it was more a case of me challenging Him. Looking back on my faith journey, I have come a long way in my walk with Him. And yet, there are still some pockets of resistance in me. Occasionally, I find that I resemble more of a defiant, rather than a compliant child. I have paid dearly for giving into my willful, fleshly old nature as I withheld forgiveness from people who have hurt me, judged others (when that is never my place), presumed to tell God that He's made a mistake, how He should handle a certain situation, or that I am not adequate for a task He has assigned to me. These are just a few of the many ways that I have limited the ability of God to bring needed changes to my life at times.

For each of us, there will always be hurdles and heartaches to overcome. Just like a runner, we can get tired and weary; we fall down and get scraped up; we can experience disappointment and discouragement. We might even hit a wall and say, "This is just too hard." However, God is right there with us: He goes before us (Deut. 31:8), He chastises us (Prov. 3:11-12), He never forsakes us (Josh. 1:5), He listens to us (Jer. 29:12), He strengthens us (Isa. 40:29-31), He beckons us to come closer (James 4:8), and to cast our cares on Him as He sustains us (Ps. 55:22).

Make no mistake about it, however. Even though it is our race to run, a race that He empowers us to run, and a race with great reward at the end, it is not just a race. It is also a battle—a very real spiritual battle.[53]

The enemy is constantly trying to pull us away from God as we are being transformed. He knows what's at stake. Not only does he not want people to be restored to a relationship with God, but when they are restored, he also attempts to steal their joy, kill their testimony, and destroy their spirit (see Job 1-2; John 10:10). He does not want us to fulfill our God-given purpose to glorify our Creator. He doesn't want us to be a testimony to others of God's grace and goodness. And he'll use extremely clever tactics to try to achieve his goal of disqualifying you from the race in any way that he can. Some such subtle strategies include (but are not limited to): doubt, guilt, pride, resentment, discouragement, and laziness.

Pride is one of his most useful strategies, as he tries to trick us into believing that we are doing it on our own strength or that if we can't run the race according to our expectations, then there's no point to it.

Even though God does expect His children to comply with a vast array of His commands, as we run our race, we must keep focused on the knowledge that: (1) they are doable, not unreasonable; (2) beneficial, not harmful; and (3) are necessary, not arbitrary. Dr. Larry Crabb, in his book, "Inside Out" warns, "When the battle is fought by trying hard to do all the Bible commands, eventual defeat is guaranteed. Either we'll slip into defeat and frustration, or we'll become stiff and self-righteous in our disciplined

---

[53] See 2 Tim. 2:3; Eph. 6:12.

conformity to standards, unable to relate deeply to anyone, including God."[54]

I believe the point being made here is that no victory can be achieved on our own strength. For in this battle, if we are legalistic in our thinking, then we are still under bondage to the law. The law is there to convict us of sin, but it is by God's grace that He covers our sin and conforms us into His likeness. When God tells us in His Word to "Be perfect," He is saying that we must allow the Holy Spirit to perfect us, not that we must keep trying harder to improve ourselves more and more. The futility of such a mindset (to keep God's perfect law perfectly every day and in every way) is much like being the proverbial hamster on a wheel—always going somewhere, but never getting there.

Paul speaks to this in Galatians chapters 3 and 5. In chapter 3 he asks, "After beginning with the Spirit, are you now trying to attain your goal by human effort?" (v.3b). At the beginning of chapter 5, he emphasizes our freedom in Christ and that with regard to the law, we are not to be "burdened again by a yoke of slavery" (vv. 1-2). Our freedom was costly—paid for with the precious atoning blood of Jesus Christ. So why would we choose to be enslaved once more to the very bondage from which Jesus died to set us free?

Clearly, the enemy has devised numerous ways to try to keep us from becoming all that we can be in Christ. Paul offers us a personal testimony of being onto the enemy's scheme in 2 Corinthians. Paul endured many hardships as a believer (2 Cor. 11:23-28), but the only time he indicates that he actually cried out and asked

---

[54] Dr. Larry Crabb, *Inside Out* (NAVPRESS, 1984), 114.

God to remove the hardship was with regard to an unnamed "thorn in the flesh." Even though we don't know the "what," we are told the "why":

> *To keep me from becoming conceited because of these surpassingly great revelations, there was given me a thorn in my flesh, a messenger of Satan, to torment me. Three times I pleaded with the Lord to take it away from me. But he said to me, "My grace is sufficient for you, for my power is made perfect in weakness."*
> *2 Corinthians 12:7-10*

God's grace is indeed sufficient—for our faults—for our failings—for our lack of faith. He has done His part in miraculous ways that we will never fully understand in this present life. Certainly, we too have a part to play in our transformation. However, our part is far easier than the part of the One who made grace possible for us. Our part is simply to say "yes" to God. We will explore more about what our part encompasses in Part 4.

Although He asks us to say "yes" to hiding His Word in our hearts, for example, He doesn't expect us to memorize the entire Bible. When He asks us to say "yes" to studying His Word, He doesn't expect all of us to become Bible scholars. When He asks us to take up our cross daily, He doesn't mean for us to walk the same path that Jesus did at Calvary—nobody could. Much of what God asks us to do for Him is part of the purifying process to prepare us for when we meet Him in glory to exalt His holy name for all eternity.

> *No discipline seems pleasant at the time, but painful. Later on, however, it produces a harvest of righteousness and peace for those who have been trained by it.*
>
> *Hebrews 12:11*

1. Read Romans 12:1-2. In what ways do we impede our own transformation at times? How much blame can we assign to the enemy at such times? How much responsibility should we own up to ourselves for our failings?

2. List some of the safeguards and incentives we are given in God's Word to help us to cooperate fully with the Spirit in the transformation process:

PART 3

OUR HEART

CHAPTER 14

ABIDE

I am the vine; you are the branches.
If a man remains in me and I in him,
he will bear much fruit; apart from me
you can do nothing.

John 15:5

In my very first class as a student in Seminary Extension years ago, my teacher told me, "If you don't remember anything else in all these classes you take, remember that the bottom line is to abide in the Vine. It's more about right being than right doing. This one truth is the most important; all else is secondary." That very wise teacher impressed on me just how vital it is to always stay connected to God. Otherwise, whatever information I learn or whatever I do in His name is in vain.

Even having that concept deeply etched in my mind and heart, being a type A personality, I still need a reminder from the Lord from time to time, when I can get so busy doing for Him, that I don't always allow enough quality time just to be with Him.

In Jesus' three short years of ministry, He accomplished so much by making time spent with His Father His top priority. In Mark 1:35, we read, "Very early in the morning, while it was still dark, Jesus got up, left the house and went off to a solitary place, where he prayed." This was both the theme and the secret to the success of His ministry. And in His final hours before being arrested, as He faced the inevitability of what was to come, in anguish, He yielded to His Father's will as He prayed in the Garden of Gethsemane. From this time of intimate communing with the Father, He drew strength to endure the cross.

In stark contrast, His disciples slept nearby. At one point, Jesus came back to where they were, trying to help them understand the gravity of the moment as He says, "Watch and pray so that you will not fall into temptation. The spirit is willing, but the flesh is weak" (Matt. 26:41). After He goes off to pray alone to the Father again, He comes back and finds them asleep once more. The consequences of their failure to stay alert were that they missed precious time to pray with and support Jesus in His hour of greatest need and were caught off guard as the soldiers came to arrest him. In the aftermath of His arrest, they fled in fear and did not respond accordingly with what Jesus had taught them and shown them by example.

Just like the disciples, we can miss opportunities to respond to situations in a manner that honors God and benefits us. We needlessly forfeit peace of mind, wisdom, and confidence, when we haven't spent sufficient time with the Father.

Despite the vast amount of needs of the people clamoring for His attention, Jesus never gave into the "tyranny of the urgent." He knew what was most important. He knew that the source of His strength came from His Father. The following poem speaks to our highest priority as we meet our daily "to do" list:

What Did You Do Today?

When daylight comes and you arise
to do the Father's will,
Do you gladly meet the needs
He's called you to fulfill?

So many things are on your list,
you cannot do them all—
Which are the most important tasks
in deference to His call?

Work and chores are piled high,
they clamor for your time;
to take on more than these is
too steep a hill to climb.

You pray, "Oh Lord, I'm burdened,
by all the things I have to do;
I start with good intentions,
but I fail to follow through."

Yet Jesus, when He walked the earth
took His load in stride;
He called upon His Father—
the key was to abide.

A caring smile, a kindly word
was what accomplished much,
to bring hope to the lost
that they might know His healing touch.

> *So as you go about your day*
> *remind yourself of this: God gives*
> *the grace for all you need to do His "to*
> *do" list.*[55]

In John 5:19-20, Jesus confirms that we must rely on God and not ourselves, as He says, "The Son can do nothing by himself; he can do only what he sees his Father doing, because whatever the Father does the Son also does." Further, He goes on to say that we will do even greater things than Him because He was going to the Father (see John 14).

How is this possible? You ask. Jesus and the Father are one, just as He prays in John 17 that we are one in them. As we abide in Him, we are given all that we need to accomplish His will in our lives (2 Cor. 9:8). His strength, power, wisdom, grace, and mercy are *all* ours for the asking as we continually seek His face.

On the contrary, those who say they love God but don't abide in the Vine, can be easily misled by the error-filled teachings of false prophets, fall completely away from following Him, or become lazy and unproductive. These are the ones whom Jesus compares with a bad tree that produces no fruit and is cut down and burned up (Matt. 7:17-20). Also, those doing works without faith are doing works in vain.[56]

Some may ask, what exactly does "abiding in the Vine" entail? Abiding in Him—to walk in intimate fellowship with Jesus— involves listening to His still, small voice through prayer and meditation. It is not a monologue of

---

[55] Monica Burney, *What Did You Do Today?*

[56] James 2:20.

listing a litany of needs and dictating directions to God. Rather, it is listening, confessing, repenting, trusting, praising, worshipping, yielding, meditating, and interceding. It is also being submerged in His Word.

When Jesus was sent into the desert, where He fasted for forty days and was tempted by the devil, it is a certainty that He prayed all throughout His time of testing. He was not only "full of the Holy Spirit"[57] and relying on the Word of God, but He was constantly communing with the Father as part of the intimate unity alluded to in John 17.

This wasn't merely a habit of going to His Father when He could "fit it in" or when He was in crisis. As we observe His relationship with His Father, we see the epitome of what it means to deeply abide in the Vine. Luke 5:16 further illustrates this as we are told that "Jesus often withdrew to lonely places and prayed."

Just prior to the day that He selected the twelve disciples, "Jesus went out to a mountainside to pray, and spent the night praying to God."[58] How often do we spend hours and hours in prayer? I know for me, it can be a challenge to pray for any extended amount of time, like many giants of the faith I've admired who spend massive quantities of concentrated time in prayer every day.

However, as I continue to mature in Christ, I have not only seen the value, more and more, of daily praying for longer periods, but also the necessity of it for my life and for the benefit of others. The greatest reward I have found is not so much in answered prayer, but the blessing of being in the presence of my Heavenly Father.

---

[57] Luke 4:1.

[58] Luke 6:12.

An acronym someone thought up years ago has also helped me and countless others to maintain a right order of things during times of prayer: **A**dore—**C**onfess—**T**hanksgiving—**S**upplication.

As we daily listen, confess, repent, show gratitude, worship, and submit to God—both in our quiet times and as we move throughout each day—we find God blessing us with more wisdom, entrusting us with more responsibility, growing us into more maturity, and our light shining more brightly for His glory.

1. Look up the word "abide" in a dictionary, as well as in a Bible dictionary. Compare and contrast:

2. Read John 15:5. Reflect on the different ways you put this verse into practice daily. On a scale of 1-10, how consistent are you to abiding in the Vine in your daily life? What areas do you consider as a strength? What areas do you believe are in need of improvement?

3. What pressures or lesser priorities might be keeping you from daily spending the optimum time with the Lord? What benefits might you receive from spending more time with the Lord than you currently do? How might God be glorified more?

CHAPTER 15

BELIEVE

*Though you have not seen him, you love
him; and even though you do not see him
now, you believe in him and are filled with
an inexpressible and glorious joy.*

1 Peter 1:8

John MacArthur once wrote: "It is no favor to God—
and no benefit to us—to like, to admire, to praise
His gospel, without accepting and obeying it. To know
the truth and not accept it brings worse judgment than
never to have known it at all."[59] He goes on to say:

> The warning here is to those who know
> the gospel, who affirm its truth, but
> who, because of love of sin or fear of
> persecution or whatever it may be, have
> not committed themselves to the truth
> they know is real. It is as if there were a fire

---

[59] John MacArthur, *The MacArthur New Testament Commentary: Hebrews*
(Moody), p. 86.

in a hotel and they are on the tenth floor. Because there is a net below the firemen are yelling, "Jump." But they do not jump. They hesitate. They are well aware of the danger and they know the net is their only way of escape; but they do not act on what they know is true and necessary. They are concerned about saving some of their possessions, or perhaps they think that somehow they can find another way out. They may be afraid of being hurt from the fall. Some might even be concerned about how they would look while jumping afraid of embarrassment. But the point is this: simply knowing about the danger and knowing about the way out of it will not save them. If they do not jump they will die. When your very life is at stake, nothing else should matter.[60]

There are some prime examples in God's Word of those who have heard the truth, but have not fully embraced it. Judas Iscariot is one of them. Here we find one who not only heard the truth, but was also a part of Jesus' inner circle. Yet in the end, he sold his soul by betraying Him and then in taking his own life, he ultimately chose separation from God rather than reconciliation with Him for all eternity. His actions revealed his heart. Hebrews 6:4-6 tells us: "It is impossible for those who have once been enlightened, who have tasted the heavenly gift, who have shared in the

---

[60] *Ibid.*, MacArthur, p. 86.

Holy Spirit, who have tasted the goodness of the word of God and the powers of the coming age, if they fall away, to be brought back to repentance."

God knew before Judas was ever born that he was not a true believer. Conversely, although his fellow disciple Peter flat-out denied Jesus in public during a brief period of sheer panic and fear after Jesus was arrested, God knew from the beginning that his heart was with Him—that he truly believed that Jesus was the Christ, the Messiah, the Son of the living God (Mark 8:29).

In John 6, we read of many of Jesus' followers who had sat under His profound teachings, witnessed His extraordinary miracles, and observed His deep compassion for people. Yet after hearing him say that they must eat of His flesh and drink of His blood, they replied, "This is a hard teaching. Who can accept it?" At that point, they walked away and did not continue to follow Him.[61]

In this same passage, Jesus tells them, "This is why I told you that no one can come to me unless the Father has enabled him." Without going into a long dissertation on the doctrine of predestination, it is quite clear in passages such as this that we are chosen from the beginning, because God knew who would love Him and who would reject Him.[62]

Many people may want to believe in Him, but get stopped by issues such as their pride or getting stuck when reading certain passages like, "If anyone comes to me and does not hate his father and mother, his wife and children...he cannot be my disciple" (Luke 14:26). Roadblocks to faith such as these can be easily

---

[61] See vv. 53-60, 66.

[62] See also John 15:16; Rom. 8:29-30; Eph. 1:4-6, 11-14.

overcome with a little time and understanding, yet many are unwilling to invest the effort it requires.

The two men described in Luke 9:59-61 were interested in following Jesus, but they were not in any hurry to do so. The one wanted to first bury his father, and the other asked Jesus for permission to say good-bye to his family. The point being made here is one of priorities: God must come first in a believer's life. If we always place other people and things ahead of God, we cannot be His disciple.

Likewise, the two thieves who hung on crosses alongside Jesus were faced with a choice: to believe or not to believe that He was who He claimed to be. In the end, the one revealed a rebellious heart as he spurned Jesus, while the other thief was repentant and surrendered to His authority.[63]

Having faith is simply *believing that Jesus is who He says he is and believing we are who He says we are.* God's Word makes clear that:

- Jesus is the Son of God (John 3:16).
- Jesus is God (Jn. 10:30).
- Jesus is the only way to the Father (John 14:6).
  Jesus is the only way to eternal life (John 11:25).

God's Word also tells us that:

- We are sinners (Rom. 3:23).
- We need a Savior (Matt. 1:21).
- We must confess Jesus as our Lord to be saved (Rom. 10:9-10).

---

[63] Luke 23:39-43.

- Believers are God's children and can look forward to an eternal inheritance (Rom. 8:16-17).

We are told in Galatians 3:6-7, "Consider Abraham: He believed God, and it was credited to him as righteousness." Understand then, that those who believe are children of Abraham." Romans 4:23 further confirms this as it states, "The words 'it was credited to him' were written not for him alone, but also for us, to whom God will credit righteousness—for us who believe in him..." What a rich heritage and amazing inheritance we have!

Like Abraham, we simply believe God is the one, true God and we obey Him because we believe in Him (2 Cor. 4:13-15). As a result, we are afforded so many benefits and blessings—one of the first being that we are seen as righteous in His eyes—our sins are completely covered by the atoning blood of Jesus (2 Cor. 5:21).

And this is his command: to believe in the
name of his Son, Jesus Christ, and to love
one another as he commanded us.
1 John 3:23

At the very moment we believe, we receive His Holy Spirit. From that point on, we have a Counselor, a Comforter, and a Friend who guides us and who convicts our hearts of sin-riddled areas so that we may be transformed more and more into Christlikeness.

We have now also become "Christ's ambassadors" who seek to help others to know Him (2 Cor. 5:20). In so doing, we will encounter hard hearts along the way, and it can be tempting for us to succumb to the belief that there is only a certain "type" that can be saved. Yet all we need to do is look at Saul (Paul) or Matthew or the sinful woman or the centurion at the foot of the cross to see that we cannot write off anyone as being beyond the reach of God's grace.

After all, we were also once His enemies and far from Him.[64] So even if we may find it hard to believe that people in prison, avowed atheists, or those who subscribe to other belief systems could be saved, like us, they too need a Savior. They also have the potential to receive Jesus, if we would only dare to share our faith with them and pray, believing for their salvation.

We will explore this topic in greater detail in chapter 22, but as we conclude this section on believing, we must briefly address the often-asked question, "How can you believe in something or someone you cannot see?"

It is a legitimate question that has been answered in a variety of ways over the span of time. Some have answered, "Well, you never actually saw a man walk on the moon, and yet you know men have." Or, "You can't see the wind, but you know that it's there." Or, "You can smell different scents in the air, like perfume or food cooking, and though you can't actually see those scents, you can see the bottle of perfume or the food frying in the pan and can trace each scent to its origin."

We can believe Jesus is real because, among other things, there is historical documentation of His existence (for example, Josephus, the ancient secular historian provides some such evidence). In Hebrews 1, we are told, "The Son is the radiance of God's glory

---

[64] See Eph. 2:13; Col. 1:21-22.

and the exact representation of his being, sustaining all things by his powerful word."

We can believe that God is real because Romans 1:20 tells us, "For since the creation of the world God's invisible qualities—his eternal power and divine nature—have been clearly seen, being understood from what has been made, so that men are without excuse." We can also believe it because scores of His prophecies have come true (some to the exact day), such as Israel becoming a country again in 1948.[65]

Atheists and skeptics alike can find many excuses not to believe. However, as has often been said, it takes much more faith to subscribe to an alternative understanding about how the world was made, or how it sustains itself, or how we came to exist than it does to believe in a loving Creator who has a purpose and plan for every individual.

Charles Swindoll is among many theologians who point out just how perfectly and magnificently the earth was created:

> The sun is 12,000 degrees Fahrenheit. All of the earth's heat comes from the sun. We are 93 million miles away—just the right distance. If the earth's temperature were an average of 50 degrees hotter or cooler, all life on this planet would cease to exist.

---

[65] See Ezek. 4:1-8; Dan. 9:24-25; Mic. 2:12-13.

Further, he points out:

> This planet rotates 365 times each year
> as it passes around the sun. Suppose it
> rotated 36 times instead? Well, our days
> and nights would be ten times as long—
> we'd be terribly hot on one side and
> unbearably cold on the other... and life
> would begin to disappear. By chance?[66]

Any reasonable person who is willing to open themself up to the possibility of an intelligent designer will find it not just comforting to know there is a Creator who can be known personally, but that the evidence for this view will show itself to be overwhelmingly in favor of a divine Being. A cross-section of many famous people such as renowned scientists Albert Einstein and Blaise Pascal, beloved authors C.S. Lewis and J.R.R. Tolkien, actress Mira Sorvino and guitarist Brian Head Welsh (from the band "Korn"), are all examples of people who were formerly avowed atheists who came to believe in God.

When Paul and Silas experienced a tremendous earthquake while in prison, all the prisoners were suddenly released from their shackles. The jailer, fearing the worst in that moment and threatening to take his own life, was reassured by Paul's words, 'Don't harm yourself! We are all here!" (Acts 16:27).

In that moment, the jailer had witnessed God at work and asked, "Sirs, what must I do to be saved?" That night, he and his family were baptized and "he

---

[66] Charles R. Swindoll, *The Finishing Touch* (WORD Publishing, 1994), p. 373.

was filled with joy because he had come to believe in God—he and his whole family" (v. 34).

Believing in God is harder for some than others because it means relinquishing control. It means trusting a Being that always was. It means trusting in a sinless Savior that endured the unspeakable for love's sake—for our sake. It also means believing in a mysterious Helper who, though invisible, is ever-present.

However, for those who do believe, God's grace is irresistible, His blessings are bountiful, all things become possible, and earth's sorrows become purposeful.

> *Now faith is being sure of what we hope for*
> *and certain of what we do not see.*
> *Hebrews 11:1*

1. Read Matthew 19:16-26. Why do you think it is hard for some people to trust Jesus as their Lord and Savior? What roadblocks do you observe in the lives of some of your unsaved family and friends? Aside from praying for their salvation, what can you do to help remove the obstacles from their path?

2. Read Acts 16:25-34. How did Paul and Silas' attitude in prison contribute to the jailer's conversion experience *prior* to the earthquake? How did the jailer's newfound belief in God contribute to his family's coming into faith? As a believer, how does your lifestyle witness help prepare the soil for harvesting souls?

CHAPTER 16

RECEIVE

Yet to all who received him, to those who believed in his name, he gave the right to become children of God.

John 1:12

First Peter 1:3-9 clearly lays out our faith journey in a nutshell. As we believe and receive Him into our hearts, we become a new creation. We receive salvation as our souls are spared from being eternally separated from our Creator. Along with that salvation, we receive the precious gift of grace, which covers over our sin-blemished lives. We receive an imperishable inheritance as children of God—one we have yet to fully comprehend. We also receive tests that are strategically designed to purify our faith, as well as a final test in eternity to reveal how completely we have yielded to God's will.

Salvation

Many come to Christ during their childhood and have the blessing of walking with Him all of their lives. Others come to Christ a little further on in their life's journey. Still, others come to a saving knowledge of Jesus on their deathbed.

For some who come to believe at an early age, they may become complacent about their salvation and not keep the fire stoked through intimacy with the Father and fellowship with other believers. The result of such a faith is described in Matthew 5:13, "You are the salt of the earth. But if the salt loses its saltiness, how can it be made salty again? It is no longer good for anything."

For those who daily fan the flame of their faith—who fully embrace the white hot heat of the purifying process—they leave behind not only a radiant testimony of a changed life, but one that God has significantly used to help transform many other lives.

People who come to faith a little later on in life can still have a powerful testimony as they walk in obedience and as they allow God to use their previous life experiences (even the poor choices they've made) as an opportunity to share God's redeeming love with others. Apostle Paul certainly did, as he attests in 1 Timothy 1:15-17. Formerly, he believed that he was pleasing God by persecuting Christians, but when he was brought into the light of God's truth, he went on to become one of the greatest ambassadors for Christ of all time.

Others come to a saving knowledge of Christ in their dying days—even in their final moments. It could be tempting as believers to focus on the unfairness of someone being allowed into heaven who had been an unrepentant sinner all of their lives, when others (like the "good" son in the parable of the prodigal son), have been faithful all along. However, this parable (along with the parable of the workers in the vineyard—Matt. 20:1-16) shows us that there is no favoritism with God.[67] We, too, should not show bias, but rejoice whenever someone comes into salvation—no matter how ungodly their past.

Although the offer of salvation is available to all, in the end, many will perish because of their hard hearts. For those who are saved, we not only have been given the gift of salvation, but we have also been given the privilege of testifying to the miracle of His redeeming love and marvelous grace.

Grace

Over time, scores of people have sung the familiar song, *Amazing Grace*—most often, at a worship service or a memorial service. Those who walk closely with the Lord have a clear understanding of this gift of grace and see it as one of God's greatest treasures.[68] However, many sing this song about God's grace without really comprehending its intended meaning for their lives. Even though Titus 2:11 reminds us "grace...that brings salvation has appeared to *all* men" (*emphasis mine*), we must do more than sing songs about His grace to see to it that "no one misses the grace of God."[69]

In Chapter 6, we looked closely at Paul and his humble response to God's lavish grace. As recipients ourselves, we recognize that even though it is a free gift, we still bear some responsibility in receiving it.

---

[67] Acts 10:34.

[68] John 1:16-17; Titus 3:7.

[69] Heb. 12:15.

- We must receive it with humility and a grateful heart.
- We must not dishonor the Giver of the gift by claiming any right to it or having earned it in any way (Eph. 2:8-9).
- When we receive it, we learn to disavow worldly ways and live godly lives (Titus 2:12).
- We are expected to continue to grow "in the grace and knowledge of our Lord and Savior Jesus Christ" (2 Pet. 3:18).
- We are called to testify to the gift and the Giver, as it is available to all who will receive it.

Inheritance

Not only do we receive immediate and numerous benefits from receiving salvation in this life, but we also will receive eternal rewards in heaven. Although we do not have any idea just exactly what they will be, we can anticipate that they will be glorious. However, God gives us some clues as to who will receive which rewards.

In 2 Timothy 4:7-8, Paul speaks of "the crown of righteousness." He prefaces his mention of this crown by stating that he has been faithful, that he did his best to obey God in fulfilling his earthly mission. He states that all those who live in obedience to God will receive this particular crown.

Another category of recipients is for those who go the extra mile, that is, those who go above and beyond that of the average believer. They may do more, give more, sacrifice more, or a combination of all of these. The reward for this category of believers is to receive an "imperishable wreath"—also known as the "victor's crown" (1 Cor. 9:24-27 NASB).

The "crown of exultation" (1 Thess. 2:19-20 NASB) is meant for the ones who fearlessly and tirelessly share the gospel. Even though Paul received great earthly joy in seeing many come to faith, he alludes to a still greater joy in heaven for leading many to the foot of the cross for salvation.

Still, another specific category is reserved for those who are pastors, elders, and teachers of the Word. In 1 Peter 5:1-4, we learn of "the crown of glory that will never fade away." God will one day give a special recognition to all of those who lovingly and diligently disciple those entrusted to their care.

Paul also talks about "the crown of life" (also referred to in Revelation 2:10 as the "martyr's crown"). This crown will be presented to all who suffered greatly for the cause of Christ. Anyone who was persecuted or endured significant pain of any kind as a result of testifying for Christ will receive this honor.

As we receive one or more of these crowns, we will no longer be tempted to keep any glory for ourselves. Along with the twenty-four elders mentioned in Revelation 4:10-11, we will most assuredly give all praise and glory to God and lay our crowns before Him at His throne.

Despite our curiosity about these rewards (wonderful as they will be), they will not compare with the exhilaration we will know when we come into glory. We will finally be home! We will worship our Creator, along with the host of heaven, for all eternity. We will be in our glorified bodies—no more pain, scars, or flaws.

And, of course, we also presently look forward with great anticipation to when we are reunited with many of our loved ones again. In addition, as we read Revelation 21, we try to imagine how magnificent it will be to see streets of gold, walls of precious gems, and gates of pearl. Yet as impressive as it will be to witness such a glorious sight, more than likely, we will be completely overwhelmed and overjoyed at being in His holy and everlasting presence—having been instantly and completely changed into His likeness (1 Cor. 15:52; 1 John 3:2).

Tests

While on earth, we receive a variety of tests in order to help us to be molded into Christ's character. With every test we fail, God gives us yet another opportunity to get it right. He often uses other people or allows a difficult crisis to come our way to get our attention and help us to put our faith in and our focus on Him.

He also disciplines us as needed, to conform us to His will and His ways. Proverbs 3:12 assures us that this discipline is for our own good.

Discipline (whether God directed or self-directed), is never fun. Corrective discipline (as God gives) is necessary for us to learn, grow, and conform to His holy standards. Self-discipline requires patience, perseverance, and endurance. The author of Hebrews talks about this in passages such as chapter 12, verses 1 and 11. To run our race for Christ in this life, we must "endure hardship as discipline" (Heb. 12:7).

Paul's frequent comparison to a runner or athlete is meant to prepare us for the grueling, rigorous training we must undergo in running our race and finishing strong. First Corinthians 9:25-27 sheds some light on what is required to finish well: going into "strict training" (v. 25), staying in our lane by not "running aimlessly," and making our body our slave (v. 27).

At the end of our earthly tests, however, we will receive the prize. The prize may include some of the rewards mentioned in the previous section. It also includes the ultimate, most satisfying prize—to hear the words that make all the tests and trials in this world worth it: "Well done, good and faithful servant!...Come and share your master's happiness!" (Matt. 25:23).

When we do reach heaven on that glorious day, we will watch as our Heavenly Father tests the elements upon which we laid a foundation while on earth. If our priorities, our time, our spiritual gifting, and our financial and material resources were all used wisely, it will be like gold refined by fire. This foundation will endure and be richly rewarded. The foundation of hay, wood, and stubble, however, laid by lazy, greedy, vain, or otherwise unfaithful servants, will be consumed by the fire. These servants will miss the blessing of receiving a reward, due to a lack of effort (see 1 Cor. 3:10-15).

Additionally (and astoundingly, I might add), God's Word contains over 7,000 promises to His children! Suffice it to say that we do not lack for anything as sons and daughters of the King of Kings. For one thing, we instantly have access to Jesus (Col. 1:27), the Holy

Spirit (Rom. 5:5), and God's truth (Jer. 31:33), the very moment we receive Jesus into our heart.

We are also promised that we will receive His guidance, protection, and provision as He goes before us, walks beside us, fights for us, intercedes for us, and as He delivers us.[70]

As if all these blessings were not enough, in Matthew 21:22, we are given the blessed assurance that if we pray in faith, God will grant whatever we ask. To a skeptic, this promise sounds incredulous. "Really? We will receive *whatever we ask*?" However, the reality of this promise must be understood in light of God's character.

For example, would He grant a request that in any way conflicts with His Word or is not asked for with right motives? No. Would He grant a request that is not in our best interest or that may bring harm to another? Again, and emphatically, a resounding "no."

God unconditionally loves us, but like earthly parents, He also puts conditions on many of His promises. When God gave us the promise in Joshua 1:5 that He would never leave us or forsake us, that was an absolute promise from our loving heavenly Father to His children—no conditions. However, when it comes to certain other promises, He does, in fact, place conditions on them. Take, for example, in 2 Chronicles 7:14, when He says:

> *If My people, who are called by My name*
> *humble themselves and pray, and seek My*
> *face and turn from their wicked ways,*

---

[70] Deut. 31:8, 1:30; Isa. 52:12; Rom. 8:34; Heb. 7:25; 2 Cor. 1:9-10; 2 Tim. 4:18.

> *then I will hear from heaven, will forgive*
> *their sin, and will heal their land.*

Notice that He specifies that only His children ("My people") are the beneficiaries of the promise. Next, He proceeds to set conditions on the promise—that He will assuredly deliver on His promise, but only after His conditions are met. Lastly, He declares the details of what He has promised.

Many of God's promises are universal and apply to all believers. Some promises are personal promises to individuals. Take Moses, for instance. He received a personal promise from God with regard to leading his people to the Promised Land. However, in his case, God illustrates how if a condition is not met, He may alter or even nullify the promise. God made good on His promise, but the promise was modified when Moses failed to adhere to God's condition to "treat [him] holy in the sight of the sons of Israel" (Exod. 3:17; Num. 20:6-13). Although Moses nearly completed his commission to lead his people into the Promised Land, he had to stop just short of reaching it—as he was forbidden from entering the land itself, due to his disobedience.

God delights in giving good gifts to His children. He wants to bestow on us all the blessings heaven can offer. Even at times when He appears to be silent and it seems as though our prayers will go unanswered, He *always* answers our prayers in His sovereign timing and perfect way—whether His answer is "yes," "no," or "not now." We must keep in mind whenever His answer is "no," that His primary objective is to use whatever means possible to ensure that we are in alignment with His will. Staying in alignment with His will is how we experience His perfect peace and bring glory to His name.

It is worth a brief glimpse back into chapter 10 to highlight one of the more valuable promises we receive as believers—the gift of wisdom. It helped Moses as he bravely led the pilgrimage out of Egypt, through the wilderness, and to the outskirts of the Promised Land. It guided David as he boldly commanded many battles on the field, as well as navigating through his own personal battles. It also aided Paul through his many extreme hardships. And it leads us along the path of righteous living until we reach our eternal destination.

Finally, in addition to the many kingdom privileges and promises that are ours to enjoy, receiving the comfort and confidence that comes from experiencing God's faithfulness, time after time, is a benefit of epic proportions.

1. Think back to the point when you first came into faith in Christ. As you received His gift of salvation, what were some of the immediate changes you made in your thinking? In your lifestyle?

2. Think about what your life is like now. What are the most significant changes in you that you are aware of, since first coming to Christ? Ask someone who has known you a long while to share what changes they have seen in you since your point of conversion.

3. Aside from the gift of salvation, list a few of the other precious gifts you have received from God. How have these gifts made a difference in your life?

CHAPTER 17

OBEY

This is love for God: to obey his commands.
And his commands are not burdensome.

1 John 5:3

I have been walking with the Lord for the better part of forty-five years now. In the course of that span of time, my life experiences have borne out the truth and reliability of God's Word. I have known the joy and fulfillment that comes from serving and testifying for Him and the soothing peace and comfort of His nearness—especially during times of grief. Further, the wisdom and discernment He has supplied in times of decision, as well as experiencing the searing sorrow and the accompanying loving correction that comes from disobeying my "Abba Father."[71]

By now, some areas of my life look quite different than the once did in the infancy of my faith: I am less selfish and more willing to put other's needs ahead of my own; more patient with others—focusing more on

---

[71] Rom. 8:15.

their attributes than on their flaws; more trusting in God as I step out of my comfort zone to take on challenging roles and assignments; and I am less fearful in other areas, as well. Yet I still struggle to relinquish control in some aspects of my heart and mind. I still have "wrestling matches" with God from time to time, even knowing that I must surrender to His will, or lose out—lose out on peace until I do surrender—lose out on the opportunity to be a credible testimony to others and—lose out on some of the sweet intimacy I experience with Him when I do fully comply to His will.

Just as we are called to honor our earthly father, we should honor our heavenly Father all the more, because He is our Creator, our Sustainer, our Redeemer, the Lover of our souls. He is the One who not only gives us life, but gives us abundant life; and not only abundant life, but life everlasting.

We are adopted into God's family the very moment we first believe. With that extraordinary privilege, comes the responsibilities that go with it—the first and foremost being to, "Love the Lord with all [our] heart and with all [our] soul and with all [our] mind and with all [our] strength" (Mark 12:30), and secondly, to "Love [our] neighbor as [our] self" (Lev. 19:18). God, our Father, who has often been characterized by the unknowing and the unrepentant as unloving, unmerciful, arbitrary, even cruel, is the same Father who, "did not spare his own Son, but gave him up for us all... [and] graciously [gives] us all things."[72]

Yet when we compare and contrast the behavior of Christians to these unknowing and unrepentant

[72] Rom. 8:32.

hearts, we come to realize that our individual disobedience as Christians significantly contributes to the
corporate failure in the Body of Christ to testify to the
correctness and blessedness of kingdom living to the
world around us.

According to a *2002 Barna research report,* "the
people who are least likely to divorce are atheists,"
but "conservative Christian faiths (defined by *Barna*
as 'born-again'), have the highest divorce rate—
twenty-seven percent." Further, twenty-nine percent of Protestants think divorce is morally wrong.
Coincidentally, their divorce rate is also twenty-five
percent. However, a more recent article in Focus on the
Family disputes these statistics. The article espouses
the fact that "nominal Christians" are lumped in with
"practicing Christians." Practicing Christians practice
their beliefs, therefore, they should not be counted with
the "nominal Christians," who only occasionally attend
church and do not necessarily ascribe to every tenet
of the faith.[73]

Yet to the secular world, Christians aren't compartmentalized into different categories. To them, we are all
just Christians (and, as mentioned previously), many
lump Christians together and label them all as being
hypocritical). So, as a believer in Jesus Christ, we are
compelled to adhere to God's commands, by surrendering daily to His will. However, to some degree, this
responsibility encompasses more than just us. When
we become a part of the family of God, we become
accountable to one another. We are called to pray for

---

[73] Glenn T. Stanton, *Divorce Rate in the Church—As High As the World?* (www.
focusonthefamily.com/marriage/divorcerate. 8-15-11).

one another, encourage one another, confront one another (when necessary), and challenge each other to greater heights in our faith walk. We are all sinners, saved by grace, yet we must attempt to bridge the divide between practicing believers and nominal Christians, so that the world can get a truer picture of who Jesus is and whom He has redeemed.

In addition to the issue of divorce among Christians, an ever-increasing number of unmarried Christian couples are living together and are not being confronted in love to repent by the leaders of many churches. Already pervasive in our current culture, abortion is running rampant among Christians as well. Alcohol, drug, and sexual addictions among believers are also continuing to increase and are reaching staggering numbers. Eating disorders have also now become more common. Long-standing church doctrines and practices are being compromised to fit the current culture of political correctness.

As the Body of Christ, we need to continually examine our witness to the world. As the late Reverend Billy Graham once said, "We might be the only Bible some people ever read." Along with that, our thoughts, words, and actions should produce more and more joy, rather than increased sorrow in the heart of our loving Father, who longs to see His children be "mature and complete, not lacking anything."[74]

So how do we move from doubt, distrust, and disobedience to trusting, obeying, and being radically transformed by His Spirit and His statutes?

---

[74] James 1:4.

According to Pete Scazzero, in his book, *The Emotionally Healthy Church*, "It takes work, energy, inconvenience, time, courage, solitude, and a solid understanding of the grace of God in the Gospel to grow in Christlikeness."[75] The problem is many believers today cringe or shrink back from words like "inconvenience," "courage," or "solitude." We live in a society of fast food, rapid-fire technology and overstimulation. Some will spend countless hours on Facebook, texting, or gaming, yet don't make room in their schedule for actual "face" time with God, family, or friends. Many are content to be "spoon-fed" a sermon each week, without digging into God's Word all week long as did the Bereans (see Acts 17:11). Many lack courage because they try to operate on their own strength, rather than seeking God on a daily basis through prayer and meditating on the Scriptures.

The foundations of our faith come from our knowledge of who God is and who we are in God. We certainly can learn experientially about who God is through nature, through relationships, and through our joys and our sorrows. However, God has given us our daily bread—His very words designed to speak directly to our hearts and minds through His Holy Spirit on a daily basis. When we fail to be in His Word with regularity, we deprive ourselves of the wisdom and knowledge that will guide us and bring strength and comfort through all the trials and temptations we face in our lives. When we fail to obey His Word, we miss the mark and fail to give God glory.

---

[75] Pete Scazzero, *The Emotionally Healthy Church* (Zondervan, 2003), 55-56.

In the next section, let us look more in detail at the various components that comprise our commitment to follow Him and to obey His commands, in order to fulfill our part in the covenant with God.

1. How does obeying God enhance our sense of peace and well-being?

2. How can our disobedience affect other believers in our lives? Nonbelievers?

PART 4

OUR PART

Blessed are they, whose ways are blameless,
who walk according to the law of the LORD.
Blessed are they who keep his statutes and
seek him with all their heart.

Psalm 119:1-2

CHAPTER 18

FOLLOW

"Follow me"

Matthew 9:9

W e have seen how God orchestrates some circumstances (as He did with Elijah), and at times allows calamities (as He did with Job), to shape and mold our godly character. He calls each of us to our own uniquely crafted assignments to help us fulfill our earthly commission to "Go and tell" (see Mark 16:15). When He does, like Moses, we can find ourselves balking. "Are you sure about this, Lord?" Or, "You've picked the wrong person for the job!" Or maybe, "I don't know where to begin." Yet He proves time and again that, "He who has called us is faithful" (1 Thess. 5:24). He never makes mistakes, and He doesn't abandon us when we do.

To be honest, for many, just trying to live out the basic tenets of the faith (to love God and love others as ourselves) on a daily basis can be quite an arduous effort. It can seem downright impossible at times—especially for recovering perfectionists like myself, who have often fallen into the trap of trying to be perfect, rather than let God transform me from the inside out. However, God assures us, "with man it is impossible, but...all things are possible with God" (Mark 10:27).

As we take a look at Jonah, we see the deceitfulness of his heart when he foolishly tries to escape God's call to preach to the wicked Ninevites. First, he flees from his home to Joppa, where he sets sail aboard a ship headed for Tarshish. It didn't take long for God to address Jonah's rebellion. While on the ship, God sends a storm that threatens the lives of everyone onboard. When it is discovered that Jonah is responsible for this calamity, he is thrown overboard and ends up in the belly of a giant fish. For three days and nights, he remains in the fish. Finally, with humility of heart, thanksgiving, and supplication, he calls out to God and then God delivers him out of the fish and safely back onto land.

Once ashore, he is again asked to go to Nineveh and preach to its citizens. He obeys God, preaches of God's imminent wrath, and as a result, the people repent of their sins. The king, motivated by fear, decrees that all should turn their hearts to God and plead for His mercy. The Ninevites' earnest actions cause God to withhold His judgment and all is well. Well, except for poor Jonah, who seems to suffer from short-term memory loss. God was merciful to spare him when he pleaded for his life while captive in the fish. But heaven forbid that those Ninevites should receive any mercy for their rebelliousness toward God! After all, he saw himself as a "good person," but those Ninevites were evil and undeserving of God's favor (my paraphrase of the book of Jonah).

Whereas Elijah was fearful and doubting God's protection of him from wicked Jezebel, Jonah was prideful
and angrily questioning God's decision to spare the
Ninevite people. Even as different as their situations
were, the end result was a lack of trust in God—and
each of them pleading with God to put an end to their
life. As we read passages such as these, we can so
quickly dismiss our own sinful tendencies and say, "I
would never do that!" Or, "That could never happen
to me!" The plain truth of the matter is that we all (at
one time or another) are guilty of fear, doubt, pride,
or anger—and for some, disillusionment and despon-
dency—even to the point of despairing of life.

So then, how can we ever truly live up to His holy
standards? The answer is quite simple, yet profound.
The only way we can gain victory is to keep yielding to
God, moment by moment, leaving "the perfecting of our
faith" (see Heb. 12:2) up to the transformative work of
the Holy Spirit. And, as we continually yield our will
over to His, it helps to remember our identity both as
His beloved children and fellow heirs with Christ, along
with His precious promise that "He who began a good
work in [us] will carry it on to completion until the day
of Christ Jesus."[76]

Further, this question of living up to His standards
can become troubling when we consider how many in
the watching world readily broad-brush all believers
as "hypocrites" and eagerly look for every opportunity
to prove themselves right. Even while the enemy of our
souls relentlessly uses voices in this world to attempt
to condemn us, God, in His great mercy, seeks not

[76] Phil. 1:6.

to condemn us (John 3:17-18), but to transform us into His likeness (Rom. 12:2). His standards are high, but through providing His Son Jesus as fully man (yet without sin), we have our greatest evidence that maintaining these standards is not only doable, but worth the sacrifice of our own will.

As we ponder the sacrifice of His only Son on the cross for our redemption, there is no reason or excuse we can possibly offer to God for why we should be exempt from obeying any one of His commands. He is one hundred percent faithful to us. His promises never fail. What He says, He will bring to pass. His forgiveness is absolute. His mercies are unceasing. His love is unending. Yet we squirm, complain, hem and haw, argue, stall, even flat-out refuse Him at times. In a word—we *disobey*.

Still, He is patient with us. He calls us to greater heights. He values us. He sees who we are, but knows who we can become. He has given each of us a prominent role in His kingdom and equips us with every heavenly resource to accomplish His will in our lives.

As alluded to in an earlier chapter, imagine a world where believers all lived out exactly what they said they believed. If we all did exactly what God has commanded us to do: knowing His Word, loving our neighbor, forgiving our enemies, praying without ceasing, making disciples—and so forth, I believe there would be far more believers and the world would be a much better place to live. But just because we are believers, and instantly receive a rich treasury of heavenly resources that enable us to carry out His commands when we become believers, it does not necessarily mean that we avail ourselves of these resources, because "the spirit is willing, but the flesh is weak."[77]

We can often be guilty of believing we are following His commands to the best of our ability, but in actuality, we are really only giving our nod to the commands—not carrying them out to the fullest. "Yes, I believe what you say, God." "Your Word is true." "Yes, I believe you have called me to obey you and to live my life for you." Truthfully, even though God always fulfills His end of the covenant relationship, we don't always fulfill our end. We pay lip service saying, "I will obey You in *all* things, Father." What we really mean though is those things in which we *feel* like obeying.

After all, just like Adam and Eve were tempted by the enemy, thoughts of compromise to our faith can subtly creep in, like, "Surely, God doesn't really mean "take *every* thought captive" (2 Cor. 10:5). Or, "Do *everything* without complaining or arguing" (Phil. 2:14—*emphasis mine*). Really? *Never* complain? "But God, I've had a bad day." "God, I'm so tired of living in this tiny space." "God, did you see what that person did to me? I don't deserve that." And memorize Scripture? "Lord, I know the Bible tells me to do this, but you know I have trouble memorizing anything. Besides, I barely have enough time and energy in my day for doing the bare essentials of daily life."

Being a follower of Christ means setting aside our preferences and agendas and getting on God's agenda. He did not promise that it would always be easy. In fact, He guaranteed us that it would be hard. However,

---

[77] Matt. 26:41 (NASB).

the rewards for following Him are far greater than we can ever imagine.

In a recent interview influential pastor/evangelist/ author, Francis Chan shared about his decision to move his family to Hong Kong. Just as in 2011, when he decided to move his family from their comfortable environment in Simi Valley to the Bay Area to get involved with City Impact's ministry in the Tenderloin district of San Francisco, it was a radical change for he and his family. However, the vast numbers of lives that are being impacted by such personal decisions are on a colossal scale, having wide-ranging and lasting implications.[78]

Some of us experience just a little bit of discomfort or sacrifice. Others face quite a lot. Sometimes being a Christ-follower involves extremely costly choices and painful sacrifices. Pastor Richard Wurmbrand spent fourteen years of his life in a Romanian jail for sharing his faith. During that time, he was frequently beaten and tortured. He might easily have decided to turn against God and allow a root of bitterness to take hold. Instead, he remained faithful and true to God. When he was finally released, he founded *Voice of the Martyrs*, a missionary organization that supports the persecuted church all over the world in many different ways. He paid a high price, risking his life at times, as he continually made a decision to live out his faith boldly— no matter the cost. As a result of following Jesus,

---

[78] Jay Kim, *Francis Chan and the Extraordinary Mundane* (Relevant Magazine, 1-23-20).

countless lives have been touched by his living sacrificially in obedience to God all along the way.[79]

This pattern of living is not optional. God means what He says when He tells us that to follow Him means we must take up our cross daily and die to our flesh nature. It is costly to be a follower of Jesus. However, again, the rewards far outweigh the sacrifice.

God also intended for the Ten Commandments to not be taken as mere suggestions and there are many more commands than those ten for us to obey (see appendix 1). Although some of God's directives may seem difficult to live out, extreme as they may seem, they are not unreasonable and they are not impossible to carry out. Even though we may be tempted to bargain or argue with God over them, they are non-negotiable and they are not even slightly debatable. They are given to us with our highest good in mind and given by a perfect and holy God, who demands our complete loyalty and who deserves our full cooperation.

God knows our wretched, sinful condition and He understands our deep longing to be set free from the misery our sins bring on us (Rom. 8:23). And one day, we will be completely liberated from all human weakness and suffering. In the meantime, God lovingly allows, or at times, orchestrates our daily circumstances to help us grow in Christlikeness, so that we may ultimately glorify Him in all that we think, say, and do.

---

[79] Pastor Richard Wurmbrand, *Tortured for Christ* (Voice of the Martyrs, 1998).

1. Compare Isaiah 53:2-3 with Matthew 4:18-20, Mark 2:13-14, and Luke 19:1-6. Why do you think people followed Jesus?

2. What evidence can nonbelievers clearly see that you are a follower of Christ?

3. Read 1 Corinthians 4:16 and 1 Corinthians 11:1. Aside from Jesus, who do you look up to as a role model in your life? How have they helped to shape your faith? Are you aware of anyone in your life who looks up to you? If so, what Christlike qualities do you believe you possess that they admire?

CHAPTER 19

TRUTH

Part One: Believing His Word

When you received the word of God, which you heard from us, you accepted it not as the word of men, but as it actually is the word of God, which is at work in you who believe.
1 Thessalonians 2:13

The essence of a believer's life is to believe God is who He says He is and that He does what He says He will do. Also, that we must do what He calls us to do—very simple and straightforward on the one hand, and yet, very challenging and conflicting on the other hand. As has often been noted by many over time, God made His truths so simple that even a child can grasp their basic meanings and be forever changed by them. He also made them complex enough to cause scholars and theologians across the ages to grapple with and argue over them relentlessly.

God's Word *is* clear enough that humans can understand it in basic terms such as, "Jesus loves me, this I know, for the Bible tells me so"[80] and, "I was once blind, but now I see!"[81] Yet it can also be quite challenging, even perplexing to read, as our hearts become convicted by some of the harsh realities about our fallen nature, which often compel us to make radical changes in our lives.

For some, believing God is easier than for others. Some just readily accept God's truths, taking Him at His Word without getting sidetracked by serious doubts or debates. For those who fall into this category, they can rest in the knowledge that God's Word is absolute, unchanging, and completely trustworthy. As the old adage goes, "God said it. I believe it. That settles it."

Take for example Mary, who did not have the benefit of the whole counsel of God's Word, but who had enough of God's truth in her to willingly accept her honored role as the mother of Jesus. Even though she initially responds to the angel's news of her holy commission with the question, "How can this be?" she does quickly and fully surrender to God's will.

Another biblical example that comes to mind is Noah (who built an ark as directed by God), in preparation of the great flood, when he had never before even seen a drop of rain. Then there was Abraham, who faithfully obeyed God as he laid Isaac on an altar he prepared, ready to sacrifice his son to God. For believers, these testimonies display unshakable faith.

However, at one point or another, we may find ourselves questioning God. Like Adam and Eve, we may try to look for what we believe to be a "loophole" in

---

[80] Anna B. Warner and William B. Bradbury, *Jesus Loves Me* (Public Domain)

[81] John 9:25.

not having to obey a certain command. Or, like Moses, we doubt God's choice in giving us a certain assignment because of our sense of inadequacy. Or, like Job, we momentarily question God's plans and purposes when He allows us to suffer greatly at times. And, like Peter, panicking as he began to sink (after having just experienced a faith-fortifying walk on water), we can so quickly lose our way when we take our focus off of God...even for a nanosecond.

Losing our way can be as disastrous as a distracted driver who ends up bringing harm to themselves or to others. Yet Jesus is right there alerting us to dangers and ready to buoy us up, saying, "Take courage! It is I. don't be afraid" (Matt. 14:27). God's Word provides us with plenty of inspiring stories of victory that spur us onto more faithful obedience. In addition, we have the added bonus of the Holy Spirit who gives us "checks" in our spirit.

The critical first step in becoming a believer is to acknowledge: (1) Jesus is the Son of God; (2) He died and rose again; (3) He did so to make a way for our sins to be forgiven and so that we would be able to spend eternity with Him; and (4) we are sinners in need of the Savior. Once that step has been taken, then as a believer, we must continue to choose to take God at His Word and learn to apply His truth more faithfully every day of our lives.

Today in our society, we see the negative effects of having removed God from our schools, sporting events, and many other facets of our culture. If we had not dishonored God by trying to replace Him with flawed human philosophies and standards, our world would undoubtedly still be a place where respect, honesty, integrity, and morality reigned supreme. It would be a place where the family unit would still be held in high regard. It would be a place where the rate of addictions, suicides, abortions, and divorce would be significantly reduced. It would also be a place where many health issues would not exist in people's lives. Pastor Greg Laurie makes this keen observation: "Our stress and agitation and troubled hearts come from ignoring His Word. Or it may be due to a simple lack of reading it to begin with. But the only way we will be able to bring God's Word into our lives is by taking the time to read it and think about it and meditate on it."[82]

We are not to just read God's Word, we need to know it. And not just know it, but to revere it. Not just revere it, but also reflect on it. Not just reflect on it, but to live it. And not just live it, but share it.

Hungering and Feasting

I have treasured the words of His mouth
more than my necessary food.
Job 23:12 (NASB)

Regrettably, it was a number of years into my Christian faith walk that I finally became aware of the necessity and benefits of memorizing and meditating on Scripture and studying God's Word in earnest. This was due, in part, to my not having been sufficiently discipled and disciplined, up until that point. It is alarming to think about just how many new believers are left to flounder for extended periods of time without

---

[82] Greg Laurie, *Living Out Your Faith* (Kerygma Publishing, 2006), p. 45.

being provided the discipleship that is so desperately needed. Just as an infant is incapable of feeding and caring for themselves—completely dependent on their parents to meet their every practical need—new believers need someone to come alongside them to be their spiritual parent and help them understand basic essentials of the faith and assist them as they grow stronger.

For me, it took having a very humble, caring, and committed pastor, along with his wife, investing time in me that led to my seeing some tangible fruit coming from my Christian life. Oh, I had faithfully attended church and served (to a lesser degree) for a number of years. But it wasn't until this couple generously poured into me with genuine love, and provided more intensive discipleship training that my family and I were profoundly impacted and I finally began to grow exponentially.

When our pastor's wife introduced Children's and Youth Bible Drill (a Bible memory program) to our church, it not only benefitted our daughters, but it benefitted me, as I began to see how hiding God's Word renews our minds, changes our hearts, and transforms us more and more into His likeness.

Even as our daughters did not yet grasp the meaning of some of the verses they were learning in Bible Drill, a foundation (akin to learning basic math skills or grammar) would prove very useful over time. Those many verses hidden in their hearts, even at a young age, would begin to help shape who they have become today.

While the kids were participating in Bible Drill, our pastor took the adults through discipleship courses.

However, even as I attended the adult discipleship offerings, I was challenged by our daughters learning their books of the Bible, when I, as yet, still did not know where to find a few of them myself.

He also offered a monthly discipleship time at our home for young married couples. In addition, he also paired me with other women to mentor, even as I was being mentored. This is what the Great Commission is all about—multiplying the disciples for the kingdom of God.

A pervasive mindset among many Christians is that pastors, evangelists, and missionaries alone are called to share the Good News. They are highly trained and qualified and are in a special category unto themselves. Even though some people are indeed called into full-time ministry to preach, teach, evangelize, and travel abroad to share the Good News, the rest of us are also called to "go and make disciples."[83]

Supporting foreign missionaries financially and with our prayers alone, does not absolve us from our responsibilities. We are all called to be missionaries—some are called away to distant lands, but the majority of us are designated to plant seeds of truth right where we live. As we accept our role and look around us to see whom God has brought to our mission field, we must be armed with God's Word. We don't need to know the Bible inside and out, as do many Bible scholars. We only need to have a hunger for God's Word. As we memorize, meditate on, and study the Bible, we become changed and will be used to bring change in other's lives.

---

[83] Matt. 28:19-20.

In an excerpt from her book, *The Hiding Place*, Holocaust survivor Corrie ten Boom testifies to the truth, beauty, and hope of God's Word as she recounts the profound agony and cruelty she and her sister endured while in the Ravensbruck concentration camp.

> It grew harder and harder. Even within these four walls there was too much misery, too much seemingly pointless suffering. Every day something else failed to make sense, something else grew too heavy. 'Will you carry this too, Lord Jesus?...'

Her agony was compounded, when upon moving from their temporary barracks over to more permanent quarters, she discovered that the place was infested with fleas. In desperation, Corrie cried out to her sister:

'Betsie, how can we live in such a place?'

Her sister did not give in to despair. She immediately began to ask God for help. The reply came in short order and was a teachable moment for Corrie, as God brought to Betsie's mind the passage found in 1 Thessalonians 5:15-18:

> 'Rejoice always, pray constantly, give thanks in all circumstances; for this is the will of God in Christ Jesus—'

Betsie then proceeded to name things for which they could be grateful: getting to stay together, the Bible (which they had smuggled in with them), the overcrowded conditions (so more women could hear God's Word at their Bible studies). But then, she went one too many (or so Corrie first thought), as she thanked God for the fleas.

> The fleas! This was too much. 'Betsie,
> there's no way even God can make me
> grateful for a flea.'

But Betsie repeated again those convicting words from verse 18:

> 'Give thanks in all circumstances.'
> she quoted. It doesn't say, 'in pleasant
> circumstances.' Fleas are part of this
> place where God has put us.

The fleas were both a nasty nuisance and a god-send. For the fleas kept the women's captors at bay and allowed them to conduct their Bible studies in Barrack 28 with no interference or repercussions from their captors—providing a way for many women to have hope when all seemed hopeless.

This compelling story is such a vivid example of how really knowing God's Word through the spiritual disciplines of memorizing it, meditating on it, and studying it can make all the difference in our outlook and can even bring spiritual freedom in the midst of severe oppression. Even though many people see God's Word as a way to control people in a negative way—imposing rigid rules and regulations—the Bible was actually designed to protect us and provide freedom as nothing else can.

Throughout the Old Testament, we see in passages such as Job 23:12 and Psalm 34:8, that the Bible is soul food. Yet many do not hunger after God's Word. They choose to overlook it as something that pastors and others involved in ministry need to chew on—but not them.

God's Word is a veritable feast of "the richest of foods" (Ps. 63:5). Choosing not to partake of this spiritual nourishment would be like choosing to physically starve ourselves of food. Jesus discloses to us in John 6:35, "I am the bread of life. He who comes to me will never go hungry, and he who believes in me will never be thirsty."

When we take the time to feed ourselves with God's Word, He promises that His Word will not return to Him empty. It will pay great dividends for our own spiritual maturity and for kingdom growth. As we hunger and thirst for His righteousness, we will be filled with the fullness of His love, joy, peace, wisdom, knowledge, and so much more.

> *Do your best to present yourself to God as one approved, a workman who does not need to be ashamed and who correctly handles the word of truth.*
> *2 Timothy 2:15*

1. How has God worked powerfully in your life through Bible study, hearing a sermon, or receiving His Word by some other means?

2. Read 2 Timothy 2:15. To what extent do you take seriously God's commands that we are to study, memorize, and meditate on His Word? Circle one:

Very seriously   Somewhat seriously   Not very seriously

3. What benefits are there to being a student of the Bible? What spiritual fruit have you directly or indirectly observed come from your (or somebody else) consistently studying, memorizing, and meditating on God's Word?

CHAPTER 20

TRUTH

Part Two: Hiding the Word

I have hidden your word in my heart
that I might not sin against you.
Psalm 119:11

Most Christians have a fundamental understanding of the importance of God's Word for their lives. Ideally, it is best from the very beginning of our Christian walk, to establish a daily habit of getting up every morning and putting God first and foremost in our schedule for the day. For some Christians, however, they are not taught early in their faith walk to make God the primary focus of their daily routine. They may focus on Him only briefly in the morning by way of a quick devotional reading, maybe shoot up a quick prayer to God when a need arises during the day, and depend on their pastor to "spoon feed" them each Sunday. As I mentioned earlier, to a greater degree, this described my early days as a believer.

For a well-grounded Christian, each day begins with not only a deep desire, but also a firm commitment to pursuing and pleasing God by spending a very personal, concentrated time with Him. This involves systematically studying the Bible. It also includes praying: acknowledging His greatness and graciousness through praise and thanksgiving, confessing sins (and asking forgiveness for them), seeking His direction, interceding on behalf of others, and listening for Him to speak to us. However, I must add a caveat (as I do not want to be Pharisaical in this), that in some cases, people find the end of the day is their best time to be still before the Lord—due to their work schedules or other vital responsibilities. Also, as important as it is to have a specified quiet time, abiding with God also means praying, praising, seeking, meditating, and applying biblical principles throughout each day.

One of the reasons the Body of Christ is not as effective in reaching the world with the Good News as it could be today, is that so many Christians are not practicing the essential disciplines of the Christian faith that give them the tools and treasures needed to be vibrant, victorious Christians.

In the 1960's, when God was beginning to be excluded from public schools in America, a cataclysmic shift began to erode the foundations of our Christian values as a nation and even within the Body of Christ, as a diluting of the gospel began to occur.

Our personal habits and spiritual growth affect not only us personally, but it also corporately affects the Body of Christ and those we are called to reach for Christ. We go to worship service every week, expecting to hear a direct word from God for our lives, but the degree to which we apply the truths can have little, no, or significant benefits to ourselves, as well as others. We praise Him corporately as a body of believers. We socially connect and are both challenged and encouraged by the exchange of information and the sharing of our experiences with other believers at Bible study or a prayer meeting. However, we must keep sharpened ourselves (as the "iron" Proverbs 27:17 tells us we are), in order to sharpen other believers as well.

We want to believe that we are actively pursuing His will—living out His words of truth and making an impact on those around us. It starts, though, with daily and deeply taking His Word into our hearts.

A good indicator of our spiritual vibrancy (or dormancy) as believers can be determined by our response to the following questions: How much quality time do I spend each day with God? How much time do I allow each day to reflect upon His truths? How well and how often do I appropriate His truths in my daily life? How intentional am I in my time with others to point them to Jesus? Do I regularly challenge and encourage other believers to walk more deeply with Jesus?

These are important questions to ask ourselves, in order to assess our own spiritual growth and to have a more vital eternal impact on the lives of others. If we truly believe God's Word, we will want to know more of what it says. As we know more of what it says, we come to know more of His love and His will for our lives.

This involves digging much deeper, going beyond devotionals and weekly sermons and really searching the Scriptures (see 2 Tim. 2:15). It also includes memorizing (Ps. 119:11) and meditating on them (Ps. 1:1-3).

When we do this diligently, the light of His truth will shine out from us brightly, people around us will take notice and will "glorify [our] Father who is in heaven" (Matt. 5:16 NASB).

More specifically, where memorization is concerned, well-known pastor, author, and theologian, Charles Swindoll succinctly states, "I know of no other single practice in the Christian life more rewarding, practically speaking, than memorizing Scripture...No other single exercise pays greater spiritual dividends! Your prayer life will be strengthened. Your witnessing will be sharper and much more effective...Your attitudes and outlook will begin to change. Your mind will become alert and observant. Your confidence and assurance will be enhanced. Your faith will be solidified."[84] So, what do we have to lose?

Living the Word

Do not merely listen to the word.
Do what it says.

James 1:22-23

In Romans 7:15-20, Paul confesses his struggle with doing what he knows to be the right thing to do, yet continuing to do that which he knows is not right. His struggle is our struggle. It is the daily process of dying to self (our sinful, fleshly nature), taking up our cross, and living in our new, redeemed nature. If we truly submit ourselves to the Spirit as we mature in

---

[84] Charles R. Swindoll, *Growing Strong in the Seasons of Life* (Multnomah Press, 1983), p. 53.

Christ, we know we are given the power to *sin less*, even though we will never be *sinless* this side of heaven.

We live in a fallen world, where we are already predisposed to sin, but we are also living in an atmosphere that is under the control of an evil adversary—an enemy who constantly pummels us with temptations and seeks to devour us "like a roaring lion" (1 Pet. 5:8). He hates those whom God loves. We can take heart, however, in Romans 8:31: "If God is for us, who can be against us?" God gives us a way of escape. He is all-powerful. We do not have to succumb to the schemes of the enemy by feeding our old, fleshly nature. We need only to cling to the Vine and ask for His help and He will enable us to overcome temptation.

For many believers, it can be so easy to take in God's Word and not act on it. In every church, there are usually some "bobbleheads"—those who hear the message and give a nod of approval, but don't "get out on the field" and actively participate in God's work. Hearing God's Word and agreeing with it are only part of the equation. Without putting feet to our faith and living out His Word, opportunities are missed and blessings are lost. We are daily called to be ambassadors for Christ, letting His light and love shine out to a dark and dying world.

The law was given to us to show us our sin and our need for the Savior. Even though we live in the age of grace and no longer are under the law, the law still has value for our lives. John MacArthur delineates this further by adding: "Knowing the law is an advantage only if we obey it."[85]

Sadly, in just about every church, there are those who know what the Bible teaches, yet they only pay lip service to God and to fellow believers. They do not bear out their beliefs in how they live their lives. We are cautioned in James 1:23-24: "Anyone who listens to the word but does not do what it says is like a man who looks at his face in a mirror and, after looking at himself, goes away and immediately forgets what he looks like."

Solidly living by our convictions as believers keeps us strong and true and helps us avoid the pitfalls that surround us. It demonstrates our commitment to Christ and testifies to the truth of His Word.

Jesus offers us a stark comparison between a man who builds his house upon a rock and another who builds his house on the sand in Matthew 7:24-27:

> *The rain came down ...the winds blew and beat against that house; yet it did not fall, because it had its foundation on the rock. But everyone who hears these words of mine and does not put them into practice is like a foolish man who built his house on sand. (vv. 25-26)*
>
> *the winds blew ...and it fell with a great crash. (v. 27)*

---

[85] John MacArthur, *The MacArthur New Testament Commentary: Hebrews* (Moody Press, 1983), p. 100.

As we stand secure on a firm foundation, we will bear out God's truth. When storms come into our lives, we will not be tossed about like a rag doll in a washing machine.

The surest way to hold firm in our faith and live boldly for the cause of Christ is to be both hearers and doers of the Word. As we "leave the elementary teachings about Christ and go on to maturity" (Heb. 6:1), it becomes easier to obey God, to please Him, and to be a more credible witness to the world.

1. On the average, how much time do you spend each day studying Scripture? Memorizing Scripture? Meditating on Scripture?

2. Read Job 23:12. Matthew 6:11, and John 6:33-35. To what degree do you view God's Word as essential spiritual nutrition for your daily life? Circle one:

Very essential   Somewhat essential   Non-essential

3. Read James 1:22-23. List some ways you are bearing out God's Word through acts of service. Read James 2:14-26. What is the danger of being too much of a hearer and not enough of a doer or vice versa?

4. In what areas of your life do you need to align yourself better with God's Word?

CHAPTER 21

SERVE

Never be lacking in zeal, but keep your
spiritual fervor, serving the Lord.

Romans 12:11

T he words "servant" and "service" can evoke reac-
tions, either positive or negative, to different people.
In the context of Christian service, it should elicit a
joyful, humble, and perpetual response of showing love
and devotion to our Savior and King. After all, Jesus
made the ultimate sacrifice in order that we might be
slaves to His righteousness and be set free from the
slavery of sin. Looking at Philippians 2:4-8, we can
easily find all the motivation we need to carry out our
faithful acts of service to Him:

> *Each of you should look not only to your*
> *own interests, but also to the interests of*
> *others. Your attitude should be the same*
> *as that of Christ Jesus: Who, being in very*
> *nature God, did not consider equality with*
> *God something to be grasped, but made*

*himself nothing, taking the very nature of
a servant, being made in human likeness...
he humbled himself and became obedient
to death—even death on a cross!*

Even having been given the most profound demonstration of Jesus' humility and servant's heart while fully human, we can still tend to hold back and resist Him in our daily, ample opportunities to serve Him. At times, we can be selfish, prideful, insecure, lazy, or try to justify inaction by more "legitimate" reasons—such as fatigue, stress, busyness, or a number of other barriers or limitations.

However, we are often (for the most part), without excuse. Thank the Lord that we will never have to take on the sins of all mankind as He did and be crucified on a cruel cross as He was. And thank our gracious God that He gave us a more relatable example of what it means to be a servant, as we may observe in the account of Jesus washing His disciples' feet (John 13:1-17). This simple act of humility is symbolic of the need for believers to be willing to "get their hands dirty"—in whatever form that may take to meet others' needs. His practical, loving gesture shows us what it looks like "to consider others better than [our]selves" (Phil. 2:3). It is really a matter of both mind and heart. The fact that the King of Kings came to earth not to be served, but to serve, should inspire all of us to do likewise.

If we are really honest, despite our knowledge of this completely awesome fact, we do not always feel like serving Him. So let's play a game of "What if?" for a moment. What if Billy Graham had not felt like leading the hugely impactful L.A. Crusade back in 1949? Or, what if Mrs. Oswald Chambers had never finished the much-beloved devotional *My Utmost for His Highest* because she grew tired of the project? Or, what if Bethany Hamilton (of *Soul Surfer* fame), had given up in discouragement after a shark attack claimed one of her arms? Or, what if Roger Huang (*Chasing God* author/founder of SF City Impact) allowed his insecurities to keep him from his mission in the Tenderloin district of San Francisco? I don't know about you, but I am so thankful that these men and women of faith did not refuse to fulfill God's assignments for them. Or, that they didn't fall short of fully obeying, by giving only a small modicum of effort to their tasks.

Taking it further on a layman's level—two of my areas of spiritual giftedness are serving and encouragement. One of my most dominant areas (within the spectrums of serving and encouraging), is manifested through my passion for baking. I started baking at an early age and by now have handcrafted easily over 50,000 cookies—a sizeable volume, by any measure. Overall, I have really enjoyed blessing others with the bounty from my kitchen. Yet having baked so much and so often, it can get very tedious at times.

Although there is far more to my ministry life than just baking, these acts of service have helped shape my understanding of what it means to be a humble servant. However, there are times when God prompts me to bake for a certain person, occasion, or cause and I just plain don't feel like it. It's a hot day or there's something else I would much rather be doing, or I am just tired of baking. I know, I know. Poor thing. She *has to* bake cookies—tough assignment—right?

Over the years, I've found myself praying, "Lord, you know my heart. I believe that baking cookies is an expression of Your love for others and that is no small thing. However, right now, as I'm not feeling joyful about baking, help me give my best. Help me not to diminish the value of this task. Still, to be honest, I'd much rather spend this time doing something more lasting and impactful. I want my life to matter."

In some of these times, His voice speaks to my thoughts by way of encouragement, such as reminding me of Matthew 25:40. At other times, His response comes to me by a word of correction through a verse such as Matthew 23:12, "For whoever exalts himself will be humbled, and whoever humbles himself will be exalted."

We all hit a wall at times in our ministering for the Lord. We may give a lackluster effort by cutting corners and doing things half-baked (no pun intended). We may still carry out our acts of service, yet with a less than stellar demeanor or attitude. Sometimes our attitude needs an adjustment regarding our priorities and preferences. Pride is always lurking around the corner, either trying to puff us up or put us down.

When we are tempted to feel prideful by focusing on our significance, it is helpful for us to refocus our mind and motives on the Lord remembering: "Always give yourselves fully to the work of the Lord, because you know that your labor in the Lord is not in vain."[86]

If we elevate ourselves in our acts of service, our attitude is offensive to God. Proverbs 29:23 cautions: "A man's pride brings him low, but a man of lowly spirit gains honor." When we exalt God and remove any fleshly

---

[86] 1 Cor. 15:58.

thoughts as we serve Him, our attitude will never fail to please Him and we will not feel like we've failed in some way.

Isaiah 64:6 provides a healthy heaping of humility for us as it reminds us "all our righteous acts are like filthy rags." And yet, when we exalt God in humble acts of service, we can know He is well-pleased with us—and that is a much richer reward than any earthly accolade or affirmation we could receive.

Case in point: I previously mentioned Roger Huang. He is an amazing man of God—a trailblazer, who through his faith and obedience, has been used of God to radically transform the drug-infested, severely impoverished Tenderloin district of San Francisco. He may never reach the level of notoriety, as have others like Billy Graham. That's not the point. His life reflects humility, not a need for notoriety. His quest is to obey God—loving and serving Him by sharing God's love with the poor and downtrodden. Even so, his obedience ignited a flame that has enlarged his influence far beyond the scope of his local ministry. His testimony reflects the beautiful assurance we have found in 2 Corinthians 9:12-13:

> *The service you perform is not only supplying the needs of God's people but is also overflowing in many expressions of thanks to God. Because of the service by which you have proved yourselves, men will praise God for the obedience that accompanies your confession of the gospel of Christ, and for your generosity in sharing with them and with everyone else.*

What is most notable about this man is the degree of his faith in God. This, coupled with his humility, has resulted in him being a mountain-moving, mighty prayer warrior who has become highly impactful in kingdom service. These are key components that are essential for any of us to be truly effective in ministry.

When we are tempted to doubt God or ourselves in serving Him, it is also important to keep in mind what Henry Blackaby once said, "God does not call the qualified. He qualifies the called." God promises us that if He gives us an assignment, He will provide us with everything we need to complete it.[87] Each of us is called to serve God with our own special giftedness. If we trust Him fully, walk humbly, and pray fervently, we will never cease to be amazed at what God will do through us.

However, even though in my life of ministry, God has seen fit to use me in some remarkable ways, it would be quite presumptuous of me to place myself in the same league as iconic saints such as Billy Graham. What makes the likes of someone like Billy Graham really stand out is that he had a special calling on his life to reach some very influential people, as well as to reach massive amounts of people all over the world (often all at once), and to be a strategic standard bearer of the faith for our generation—just as were Noah, Abraham, Moses, Peter, and Paul, long before him. The truth of the matter is that we are all saints with a high calling to love and serve God by loving and serving others. We are all instructed in 1 Peter 4:10, "Each one should use whatever gift he has received to

---

[87] See 2 Cor. 9:8.

serve others, faithfully administering God's grace in its various forms."

John MacArthur, in *The MacArthur New Testament Commentary on Galatians* states:

> The validity of good works in God's sight depends on whose power they are done in and for whose glory. When they are done in the power of His Spirit and for His glory, they are beautiful and acceptable to Him. When they are done in the power of the flesh and for the sake of personal recognition or merit, they are rejected by Him. Legalism is separated from true obedience by attitude. The one is a rotten smell in God's nostrils, whereas the other is a sweet savor.

The most glorious outcome of our acts of service originates from our serving with a pure heart. If we always keep in clear view the "who" we are doing it for (the "He" instead of the "me" or "we"), our humble service will not fail to glorify Him and bless others. We must not serve God out of a sense of obligation (a works-centered mentality), but out of gratitude for His love, grace, and mercy. We could never repay our Lord for all that He has done and continues to do in our lives, but our great joy and honor is to "work at it with all [our] heart, as working for the Lord, not for men."[88]

---

[88] Col. 3:23.

1. Read Philippians 2:3-8. What is the dominant characteristic of a servant? In what ways do you see yourself still lacking in this character trait? In what specific ways does Jesus' example compel you to serve more faithfully?

2. Read 2 Corinthians 9:12-13 and Galatians 6:9-10. How can our acts of service make a difference to other believers? To nonbelievers?

3. Look up Colossians 3:17 and 3:23. What part does attitude play in our acts of service? Read Genesis 4:2b-12. To what degree does our attitude affect God's view of our acts of service?

4. Read 1 Samuel 15:22. Why is it important to keep our priorities in order when serving and sacrificing for the Lord?

CHAPTER 22

SHARE

The Great Commission

*Therefore go and make disciples of all
nations, baptizing them in the name of
the Father and of the Son and of the
Holy Spirit, and teaching them to obey
everything I have commanded you.*
Matthew 28:19-20

E ven though it would be hard to imagine that any
Christian would be completely unaware of both
their privilege and responsibility as a believer to share
their faith with others, it is very common in the Body
of Christ to encounter believers who do not regularly
share their faith with other people. The reasons for
this are varied: fear of rejection, feelings of inadequacy, unpreparedness, not a high priority, belief that
only certain people are called to evangelize, or holding
fast to the belief that being a lifestyle witness alone is
enough to be an effective witness.

When Jesus walked the earth, His Father's love sustained Him through every situation He faced. As a boy, He was blessed with God-ordained, earthly parents who helped prepare Him for His earthly mission. When He was baptized, God sent a special affirmation in response to Jesus' public declaration of obedience and trust in the Father.

When He fasted for forty days and nights in the desert, God's Word provided the nourishment, encouragement, and strength needed for Him to disarm the enemy's temptations. As He met opposition all through His public ministry, the Father amply supplied Him with wisdom, calmness, frankness, compassion, grace, and mercy to extend to others. In times of needing rest and refreshment, God met Him with ministering angels and with His own companionship.

Likewise, our gracious Father also prepares us for our earthly commission. He affirms us as we declare Jesus as Lord. He gives us strength and encouragement as we combat the enemy's schemes. He provides us with all the tools for our spiritual toolkit needed to face any form of opposition in our lives. He also promises us protection, with an army of angels at His disposal (Luke 4:10; Heb. 1:14). Yet even having been given all these provisions, it is up to us to draw on His strength through His Word, through prayer, and fellowship with other believers.

We have to put on our spiritual armor to combat the enemy. Yes, God fights for us, but we have to be active participants by knowing His truth and living it boldly. This requires studying His Word (2 Tim. 2:15), hiding it in our hearts (Ps. 119:11), meditating on it (Ps. 77:11-12), and testifying to it (Ps. 71:15-16).

When we are reminded: "The heart *is* deceitful...and desperately wicked" (Jer. 17:9 KJV) and that "there is no one who does good, not even one" (Rom. 3:12), it is mind-blowing to comprehend that He would ask us to be co-laborers with Christ as we fulfill the Great Commission on earth. Yet He continually extends mercy and forgiveness to us, calls us His children, and considers us His friends. How can we do any less than give Him our whole heart, serve Him with gladness, and obey His commands fully and faithfully?

So when we encounter verses such as Matthew 28:19-20 and Mark 16:15, we recognize indisputably that He means for us to be sharing the Good News and make disciples of others. However, we try to find ways around commandments such as these, "I don't know how." "I'm afraid of saying the wrong thing." "I need to keep studying until I feel more prepared." "I simply don't have the time." "Other people are gifted in this area; I'm not." The list of roadblocks we can put up is endless.

The first step toward fulfilling the Great Commission from a personal standpoint is to *reflect on what our salvation means to us.* It is also helpful to think back to the point of our conversion—how someone cared enough to share the greatest news in the world with us and what a difference it has made in our lives.

The second step is to *develop a burden* for the lost. Remembering our lives before coming to know Christ can be a good reminder of how desperately we all need a Savior. Praying for God to give us a heart of compassion, so that "we regard no one from a worldly point of view,"[89]

---

[89] 2 Cor. 5:16.

motivates us to reach out to others without bias and share with them how much God loves them and how He has a special purpose for their lives.

The third step is to *be prepared*. First Peter 3:15 gives us this admonition: "Always be prepared to give an answer to everyone who asks you to give the reason for the hope that you have. But do this with gentleness and respect." Being prepared means to be well-grounded in God's Word. The result produces:

- A consuming passion to share God's love (Isa. 63:7).
- Confidence that we are handling the Word of truth correctly (1 Tim. 2:15).
- Trust instilled in the one we are reaching out to that we are speaking on the authority of God Himself (1 Pet. 4:11).

There are also many resources available on how to share our faith that can help aid in building confidence and boldness in witnessing (see appendix 2).

Being prepared also means being prayed up in the Spirit. It is God who is at work in us and through us. We must seek His guidance ahead of time and as we are sharing our faith with others (and yes, it is possible to pray in the Spirit even as we are witnessing). Jesus made it clear that He could do nothing apart from the Father.[90] Whenever He reached out to others, it was always by staying closely connected with the Father that He was able to accomplish the Father's will.

---

[90] John 5:19; 8:28.

He also has taught us that as we pray, we must put His will ahead of our own.[91] We might be tempted to pray something like, "Father, help me lead that difficult person to the cross, so I don't have to suffer their offensive behavior anymore." Instead, with all humility, our attitude in prayer should be: "Father, give me a love and concern for this person who needs Jesus. Help me to forgive their offenses. Help me to share the living hope that I have with them. Amen."

The fourth step is to *be faithful in obedience* and not out of a sense of obligation. There is a distinct difference. It is an honor to bear the name "Christian." It is an extraordinary privilege to lead someone to the Lord, but it cannot be motivated by guilt or an unhealthy fear of God. Although it is a direct command from God, we should never be driven by duty, but rather, out of love for God and concern for the lost.

We also need to always keep in mind that it is the Holy Spirit's job alone to convict hearts. We cannot save anyone. We plant the seeds through spreading His Word, but it is He who redeems lives and transforms them. However, as we remain faithful in obeying His command, we will reap the blessing of seeing a bountiful harvest of souls come into the kingdom.

Romans 10:14-15 challenges us with the following questions: "How, then, can they call on the one they have not believed in? And how can they believe in the one of whom they have not heard? And how can they hear without someone preaching to them?" We cannot assume someone else will tell them. It's up to us to plant seeds and trust God for the results.

---

[91] Matt. 26:39.

Many people in oppressed countries around the world risk all to come to Christ. They risk ridicule, being disowned by their families, persecution, even risking their very lives. In America, we often shy away from sharing the gospel because we are embarrassed, we fear rejection, we lack confidence, we get complacent and lazy, or we may think evangelizing is best left to "the experts." However, we are without excuse. The Great Commission was meant for us all.

For every excuse we can offer for not testifying to the truth, there is a Scripture verse to refute our claim:

- Embarrassment: Romans 1:16; 2 Timothy 1:8-9

- Fear of rejection: Psalm 56:3-4; Galatians 1:10

- A lack of confidence: 2 Corinthians 3:4-6; 2 Timothy 1:7

- Complacency/Laziness: Romans 12:11; Colossians 3:17

For every soul that we reach out to on earth, we will receive eternal rewards. That's not to say that we should be motivated to share our faith for the rewards it may bring us. We do, however, receive tremendous joy when we introduce others to Christ.

My friend Gayle has traveled the world sharing the gospel through ministries such as *Simply the Story* and *Jesus Films*. When she is not jetting off to another country, she is locally going to parks, apartment buildings, or anywhere else she feels God leading her to share the gospel. If you asked her what is the secret to her being a successful witness for Christ, she would tell you that it's not complicated and it's not a chore. If you truly love the Lord, you will also love those "he came to seek and to save." Just get out there and share. God will be with you, His Spirit will guide you in what to say, and He will honor your efforts to obey Him.

> *The harvest is plentiful but the workers are few.*
>
> > *Matthew 9:37*

1. Why do you think it is so hard for some believers to obey the Great Commission?

2. Evaluate how often you share the "Good News" with others. Circle one:

   Often   Seldom   Never

3. How prepared are you "to give an answer to everyone who asks you... for the hope that you have" (see 1 Pet. 3:15)?

CHAPTER 23

LOVE

The Greatest Commandments
Mark 12:28-34

The Father's deepest desire is to be loved—
genuinely loved—by His child.
(from *A Heart Like His* by Beth Moore)

I think most would agree that love seems to be the most popular topic among songwriters. Tunes such as: *All You Need is Love*; *The Things We Do For Love*; *What the World Needs Now is Love; Sweet Love* all extol the virtues of love or express the deep hunger and aching of the human heart concerning love relationships.

The Bible is replete with verses that speak of God's love for us, how we should show our love for Him, and how we are to love ourselves and one another. The word *"love"* can trigger all kinds of emotions: joy, acceptance, hopefulness, sadness, pride, jealousy, and more. For those who experience God's love, they come to understand what perfect love is like. Certainly Adam and Eve knew it full well until they fell from God's grace and had to adjust to a whole new way of living and relating to God and each other.

As flawed humans ourselves, we desire to be in complete harmony with God, but always seem to fall short in some way or another. Yet Jesus set the standard for sacrificial love and showed us how it is achieved. Although He displayed a wide range of emotions as a human, He did so without sin. Despite the many difficult situations He encountered, His response always glorified God the Father. However, our desire for perfect love is frustrated by our willful nature which, when indulged, breeds sin. Sin creates a barrier between us and God, us and others, and even conflict within ourselves.

In Mark 12:30-31, we are given a clear mandate of what is expected of believers: "Love the Lord your God with *all* your heart and with *all* your soul and with *all* your mind and with *all* your strength." Secondly, we are told to, "Love your neighbor as yourself" (*emphasis mine*).

Loving God

We are given what may appear to be some pretty extreme parameters of what defines our love for God:

> *If anyone comes to me and does not hate*
> *his father and mother, his wife and children,*
> *his brothers and sisters—yes, even his own*
> *life—he cannot be my disciple.*
> *Luke 14:26*

*Unless you eat the flesh of the Son of Man
and drink his blood, you have no life in you.*
John 6:53

*Anyone who does not take his cross and
follow me is not worthy of me.*
Matthew 10:38

To an unbeliever, these words might make absolutely no sense whatsoever and may seem beyond the pale. However, to believers (especially as we grow and mature in Christ), the meaning of these words becomes clearer and clearer, making it easier to obey them. To a believer, God gives us many reasons to love Him:

- He sent His only Son to die for our sins (John 3:16).
- He loved us, even when we were still His enemies (Rom. 5:8, 10).
- God adopts us as His children (Eph. 1:5; 1 John 3:1).
- God is love (1 John 4:16).
- He is our peace (Eph. 2:14).
- He is our hope (Rom. 15:13).
- He is our help (Ps. 33:20).
- He is our light (John 8:12).
- He is our wisdom (1 Cor. 1:30).
- He is our strength (Ps. 118:14).

The true question to ask ourselves is not, "Why should I love God?" Rather, "Why should God love me?" After all, we have done nothing to deserve love and there is absolutely nothing we could possibly do to earn His love. We did not initially seek Him—He sought us first. He loves us completely, passionately, and unconditionally.

We, on the other hand, do not always love Him entirely. We give parts of our minds, hearts, and lives to Him, but may withhold from Him areas of our lives in which we want to maintain control. Sometimes we love Him passionately. Other times, we may love Him half-heartedly as fatigue, distractions, or complacency creep in. We also believe that He is the potter and we are merely the clay. Still, we presume to put conditions on what we will and will not do for Him; whom we will and will not forgive; whom we will show love toward and whom we will ignore.

When we love God "with all our heart, soul, mind, and strength" (as we are commanded to do in Mark 12:30), we receive the blessing of His favor, knowing that we are pleasing to Him and fulfilling our God-given purpose. As we die daily to our former way of life and live for Him, we experience the abundant life He has promised us.

Loving Others

At the moment we first receive Christ in our hearts, we only begin to sense how boundless is His love for us. And for those who walk closely with the Lord for many years, as they near the end of their lives, they are still discovering new depths of His love for them.

Yet even in our infancy as believers, we are amazed by His unconditional love toward us. The next step, however, is to recognize and undertake our responsibility to love others with that same sacrificial love that we have come to know.

Some people are naturally easier to love than others. However, Jesus gives us this challenge in Matthew 5:46-47: "For if you love those who love you, what reward do you have? Do not even the tax collectors do the same? If you greet only your brothers, what more are you doing *than others*? Do not even the Gentiles do the same?" (NASB).

Jesus calls us to love all people and He proved it could be done. He loved lepers—and prostitutes—and those who persecuted Him—those who betrayed Him—those who abandoned Him—and you and I.

Are we willing to do the same? Are we really willing to "get our hands dirty?" Are we willing to love our enemies? Are we willing to go beyond praying and staying in our safe, sanitized "church bubble" and come alongside people who don't look, think, or act like us—even some who might not look like they "belong" at church?

Life is messy. And some lives are really messy—downright stinky, in fact. As individual believers and as the Body of Christ, we need to risk getting close enough to them to understand their hopes, dreams, but also their pain and fears as well. Of course, at times, it requires people who are professionally trained to help work through years of dysfunction. For the most part, however, there are many "walking wounded" who really just need God's redeeming love: to heal and restore them, to correct and redirect them, to give them hope and purpose. As Christ's ambassadors, we are called to be truth-bearers, bringing the hopeful message of His life-giving truth that sets captives free.

When it comes to messy lives, I'm not just referring to those who society has deemed "the untouchables" either. I'm also talking about people whose hearts are filthy with sin. Their outward appearance may be clean and tidy, but inwardly their lives are reeking of pride, anger, guilt, or shame.

Oftentimes, the Christian response to people who are especially "messy" (or, more to the point, "messed up") closely resembles that described in James 2:15-17:

> *If a brother or sister is without clothing and in need of daily food, and one of you says to them, "Go in peace, be warmed and be filled," and yet you do not give them what is necessary for their body, what use is that? Even so faith, if it has no works, is dead, being by itself.* (NASB)

I believe this verse is not limited to meeting material needs. Certainly, there are many people desperate to have basic, practical needs met, but the greatest need of all is the spiritual hunger in people's hearts. At the core of this verse is the exhortation that we are to go beyond meaningless words and actually get involved in people's lives to point them to Jesus and help them find resources or solutions to whatever their need may be.

Several years ago, my husband and I took in a homeless person for a year. We had previously had a number of people stay at our home for extended periods of time before in our married life, but it had always been a family member or personal friend who was going through a rough patch. However, this person was someone we had known for only a short while, but also one whom we deemed trustworthy. After praying about it extensively, we knew God was calling us to this assignment.

Throughout the year, we went through many ups and downs. I learned some things about myself (as well as the human condition), as we shared our life experiences and experienced life together for a time. My faith in Jesus played an integral part of our conversations, though I tried not to be "preachy." I knew that my demeanor, tone, attitudes, and responses to situations would speak louder than any words I spoke.

I have no regrets about that chapter in my life, hard as it was at times, because I knew by my obeying God in this, that He was honored and pleased. However, even though I would accept a similar assignment, if God was clearly calling my husband and I to do it, I would not necessarily go out looking for another situation like that either. Sometimes God gives us a one-time assignment and sometimes He gives us an ongoing calling to minister in a certain way.

We are all called to love one another and that can look very differently for each one of us. We do, however, find an underlying guide as Micah 6:8 instructs us, "to act justly and to love mercy and walk humbly with [our] God." As we meet the needs of others and "go the extra mile," it will be as if doing so for Jesus Himself (Matt. 25:40). When we show love to our enemies and offer up prayers on behalf of those who persecute us, they will experience the love of Jesus. If we try to love others with our flawed, human love, we will fail every time. However, when we love sacrificially like Jesus, lives will be radically and forever changed.

Loving Ourselves

All throughout God's Word, we read of the two distinctive ways people choose to love themselves—the one honors God, the other exalts self. From the beginning of time, man has had a proclivity toward pleasing self over pleasing God. We saw it in the Garden with Adam and Eve. We saw it through their offspring, on down the line.

However, even considering man's sinful nature, there is still a deep-down human longing to be restored to harmony with God. This longing can be satisfied when reconciliation with God occurs. As we surrender our hearts to Jesus, God sits on the throne of our hearts and we are then capable of loving ourselves as God intended.

Before we examine what loving ourselves as God intended looks like, we will first look at what God did not intend when He gave the command, "Love your neighbor as yourself." Our fallen nature seeks pleasing self above God. This manifests itself in ways such as described by the Seven Deadly Sins: pride, envy, wrath, gluttony, lust, sloth, and greed.[92]

The source of these sins is rooted in selfishness—a self-will that insists that it must be satisfied above all else. Yet the quest to satisfy self is never fully achieved. The hungry beast of self-love never has enough money, status, revenge, sexual pleasure, or whatever other pleasure that will appease its desire for ultimate fulfillment.

Ecclesiastes 5:10 speaks to the craving for money, "Whoever loves money never has money enough."

---

[92] Prov. 6:16-19.

Likewise, 1 Timothy 6:10 warns that, "The love of money is the root of all kinds of evil" (KJV). There are many fleshly cravings and desires like this that Satan uses to entice people away from what is good, godly, and truly satisfying: The lust for power, the desire to pay back evil with evil, the need to be praised, the gluttony of food, wine, or one of a number of other indulgences—the list is endless.

God's Word is crystal clear about where He stands on people feeding their flesh. Colossians 3:5-6 gives us this word of caution:

> *Put to death, therefore, whatever belongs*
> *to your earthly nature: sexual immorality,*
> *impurity, lust, evil desires and greed, which*
> *is idolatry. Because of these, the wrath of*
> *God is coming.*

On the other hand, as we look at what God does intend when He says we are to love ourselves, we can rely on the Scriptures to point us in the right direction. Psalm 139 is a beautiful affirmation of how intimately God knows us and how miraculous a creation we each are. In verse 14, we are reminded how we are "fearfully and wonderfully made." He knows our every thought, word, and action before we ever conceive of them. His thoughts of us are infinite and intimately personal toward us.

Matthew 6:26-30 and 10:29-31 also reinforce how highly valued and loved we are. Although "he remembers that we are dust" (Ps. 103:14), we can rejoice in the knowledge that we are, "a chosen people, a royal priesthood, a holy nation, a people belonging to God" (1

Pet. 2:9). We are adopted into His kingdom as children of the King of Kings. We are clothed, "with garments of salvation and arrayed...in a robe of righteousness" (Isa. 61:10). If ever we find ourselves doubting our worth in this life, we can look to the truth and beauty of God's Word to remind us of just how very loved and special we are.

Only as we do keep our focus on God's love for us can we truly love and accept who we are. And only as we embrace our personality, our physical appearance, our strengths, and our weaknesses, in light of this lavish and eternal love, can we genuinely love others.

Yet many question the choices God made in making them, "Why am I so short?" "Why did you make me an introvert?" "Why can't I look like so and so?" "I don't like my long nose." "I wish I was not such a loudmouth."

However, it is never our place to presume to tell God that He made a mistake when He made us. Or, that He could have done a better job. Or, that we know better than Him. Isaiah 29:16 and 64:8 (along with Romans 9:20-22), perfectly illustrate the concept that our Creator has sole authority to say what should and what should not be.

I should think God is far more grieved than offended when His children question His choices regarding how He created them. After all, of all the vast multitudes of people ever created, there is no one exactly like us: no one has our exact DNA blueprint; no one else has our exact fingerprints; no one has the ability to think, speak, or act precisely like we do every second of every day. Certainly, though many come extremely close (such as in the case of identical twins), there is always some distinguishable difference between people. The

189

point being, He took great care to fashion each one of us just so.

When we get down on ourselves because we are not as seemingly perfect, attractive, talented, or capable as someone else, we rob ourselves of the joy God intended for us. Contrary to the world's arrogant view that only some people are "God's gift to the world," every person is God's special creation. Keeping a godly perspective in mind of who we are in Christ, we can each celebrate being exquisitely loved, and an uniquely fashioned person designed to fulfill our purpose in this world with humbleness of heart.

For those who spend any time and energy stewing, fretting, resenting, or even obsessing over their "flawed" physical features or other identifying characteristics, it can be a miserable existence.

Unfortunately, I can attest to this from personal experience, as I wasted precious time in my earlier life focusing more on my "deficiencies," rather than fully embracing all that I am. Even though (to a much lesser degree), I am still being delivered from some wrong perceptions about myself, God is changing me day by day, wanting to see me completely set free from bondage in this area. Choosing to see myself through God's eyes, allows me to love myself without indulging in arrogant or insecure attitudes about myself.

The only thing that can bring anyone with a poor self-perception back to a healthy center is to believe what God tells them is true about themself and to live it like they believe it. For many though, their insecurities will consume them and determine so much of how their lives will go. Living out a self-fulfilling prophecy (dictated solely by emotions, rather than based on truth), will always guarantee a downward spiral.

Some people, however, though they are naturally outgoing and confident, will repel or dominate others and offend God if they do not possess a humble heart. Pride is their downfall.[93] Additionally, Romans 12:16 warns us never to be proud or conceited.

Other people can actually be very insecure, yet are masters at masking their insecurities by asserting themselves to a fault. They are brash, pushy, and are grossly insensitive to others.

Again, a person whose compass points true north—who closely walks with God—will find peace and assurance in knowing their intrinsic worth. They won't need to puff themselves up or put others down to feel good about who they are. They will not insist on asserting their will, but will trust in the sovereignty of God and yield to His will—even if it means letting go of longings like cosmetic surgery to fix a physical flaw or pretending to be someone they are not.

Throughout the New Testament, Paul gives us examples of what a healthy self-perception looks like. In 1 Corinthians 15:10, we see his acceptance of who God made him. In passages such as Galatians 6:14 and 1 Timothy 1:15, we see his humility. In 1 Corinthians 4:16 and 11:1, his charge to imitate him does not originate from a prideful spirit, but from one who acknowledges that Christ lives in him (Gal. 2:20) and shines His light and love out through him.

We can never take credit for the good things people see in our lives. So, like Paul, our only boast is in

---

[93] See Prov. 11:2 and 16:18.

Christ. When we are tempted to claim some praise for ourselves, we are robbing God of the glory due His holy name. When we think we need to puff ourselves up or demean someone else to make ourselves feel better about ourselves, then we need to look at passages such as Philippians 2:6-8 and 1 Corinthians 13:4-8 to make adjustments in our thinking.

As we obey God's command to love ourselves and resemble Christ's likeness more and more, we will find that we will have less and less of a need to exalt or to berate ourselves. We will see ourselves as God sees us—clothed in His righteousness and in the radiant light of His love.

1. How do you interpret the verse from Luke 14:26 regarding hating members of our own family? How would you defend this position to an unbeliever as it applies to loving God?

2. Read Matthew 5:44-47 and Acts 10:34. How can living out these verses make a difference in someone else's life? In your life?

3. How are guarding your mind and keeping your body pure forms of loving yourself?

4. How is having low self-esteem a poor testimony as a Christian? List some ways we can encourage others who struggle with low self-esteem:

CHAPTER 24

LAW

The Ten Commandments: Part One
Exodus 20:3-12

Although Christians are well-acquainted with the Ten Commandments, there are some who could not name them all if asked. More than that, many do not recognize the degree of seriousness of some of the commandments, such as not taking the Lord's name in vain or keeping the Sabbath day holy. For the most part, however, they do obey the vast majority of the commandments. And even though many non-believers are familiar with God's overall commandments (even following some of them, like "The Golden Rule"—Luke 6:31), more often than not, they view them as merely common sense, cosmic rules that are necessary in order to live in a civilized society. They don't see them as a biblical mandate from God, nor comply with them in deference to Him as a uniquely sovereign deity.

We live in a day and age where absolute truth has swiftly given way to the popular sway of moral relativism—no right or wrong. Truth is whatever you deem it to be. Revisionist history and an increasing preoccupation with self is influencing the next generation away from the truths that we "hold to be self evident."[94] Our country was founded on the tenets of the Judeo-Christian faith to the one, true God. However, as we have moved away from God's statutes, we have lost our moral compass as a nation and are now clearly and abundantly experiencing the ramifications of our disobedience to God.

In their book, *The Ten Commandments: The Significance of God's Laws in Everyday Life,* Dr. Laura Schlessinger and Rabbi Stewart Vogel note, "In 'civil law' things are right because they are commanded—by a legislature and judicial system. In 'God's law' things are commanded; therefore, they are right. Man does not define virtue and vice; God is the arbiter of morality."[95]

Schlessinger and Vogel go on to later explain, "When the prophets chastised the people and warned them of impending divine punishment, the warning was directed toward nations as a whole and not individuals. In the biblical world, there was communal responsibility. People were responsible for the deeds of their neighbors. What a different world we live in today, when people don't care what others do wrong as long as it doesn't affect them, and when they will not speak out against immorality if it would in any way jeopardize their position or possessions." The authors further assert, "Life takes on additional meaning when we

---

[94] The Declaration of Independence (http://www.archives.gov/founding-docs/declaration-transcript).

[95] Dr. Laura Schlessinger and Rabbi Steward Vogel, *The Ten Commandments: The Significance of God's Laws in Everyday Life* (Cliff Street/Harper Collins, 1998), p. 19.

stand for something; unfortunately, today many people don't stand for anything other than personal comfort and acquisition."[96]

If we continue on this path away from God, we will not only continue to miss out on His bountiful blessings as a nation, but at some point, we will suffer His powerful wrath. In the days of Noah, God reached the point when He could tolerate evil no longer. He saved a remnant through Noah and his family, but He had to completely eliminate the remainder of His creation that had been corrupted by insidious evil.

As we read in Genesis 19 about Sodom and Gomorrah, we see that the only ones who survived utter destruction of these cities were those who obeyed the instructions to flee, to not look back, and to not stop—all others were consumed by the burning sulfur raining down from heaven (except for Lot's wife, who was turned into a pillar of salt). In the case of Pharaoh not heeding Moses' warning (given through the ten plagues), devastation came as all the first-born Egyptians (including Pharaoh's own son) were killed (Exod. 8-12).

Some people think that God is a God of hate, that He thrives on randomly punishing people and causing them to suffer, but nothing could be further from the truth. God is the Giver and Sustainer of life. He sent His only Son to us so that we "may have life and have it abundantly" (John 10:10). He does not delight in seeing a single person perish—not even the wicked. He says in His Word, "For I take no pleasure in the death

---

[96] Dr. Laura Schlessinger and Rabbi Stewart Vogel, *The Ten Commandments: The Significance of God's Laws in Everyday Life* (Cliff Street/Harper Collins, 1998), p. 194.

of anyone, declares the Sovereign Lord. Repent and live!" (Ezek. 18:32—see also 18:23).

In addition to numerous other commands in His Word, God gave us the Ten Commandments for our benefit, but even more so, that we may bring glory and honor to Him. However, from the beginning of time, man's pride has tried to supersede God's authority over him. God's gift of free will can be both a blessing and a curse. It is a blessing in that we aren't being constrained by some kind of unmerciful taskmaster or puppeteer. Yet it can be a curse when we choose to live outside the realm of God's sovereign protection. However, the choice to submit to God and His requirements (or not) is left completely up to us. Schlessinger and Vogel aptly comment:

> when it comes to Deity, there are really only two possibilities. We either acknowledge our creation in the image of the objective God revealed in Scripture, or we inevitably MAKE GOD in OUR own image.[97]

God is a jealous God. He will not share His glory with another. I believe that is why the first four of His Ten Commandments are positioned ahead of the remaining commandments. He tells us in Isaiah 45:5, "I am the LORD, and there is no other; apart from me there is no God." So either we believe Him, love Him, and serve Him, or we attempt to become our own god and face a life lacking any real meaning and a future

---

[97] Dr. Laura Schlessinger and Rabbi Steward Vogel, *The Ten Commandments: the Significance of God's Laws in Everyday Life* (Cliff Street/Harper Collins, 1998), p. 19.

without eternal hope. The blessings that come from our keeping His commands are satisfying and plentiful. The consequences of not complying with His commands are disastrous and eternally devastating (see Gen. 3:14-19).

As I eluded to earlier on, it is daunting even just to consider the enormity and complexity of all the commands of God as they apply to our personal lives—much less try to keep them all, all the time. Even though God has, in a broad sense, pared them down within the confines of the Greatest Commandments, the Great Commission, and the Ten Commandments, He still gave them with the intent for us to obey them—all of them. The law given to Moses was meant to show us our sinful nature and our need for a Savior. It was not intended to be a legalistic quest for perfection that we could never attain. What a great God we serve that He makes our freedom and protection of utmost priority.

There is not enough time in this book to go into a great amount of detail in exploring each of the Ten Commandments. However, I would be remiss if I didn't give some attention to each one.

1. *"You shall have no other gods before me." Exodus 20:3*

Not only must we not set ourselves up as a god in any way, but we are not to make anyone else into a god either. Many people are worshiped in this world, be it entertainers, musicians, athletes, and others. We can have heroes, just as long as we keep them in their proper place: beneath the realm of the one and only holy, majestic God and Creator of the universe.

When Paul says in 1 Corinthians 11:1, "Be imitators of me, just as I also am of Christ," he is not setting himself up as a god, as a cult leader, or a false prophet. What he is saying is that the good people see in him is Christ who lives in him. This humble "chief of all sinners"[98] is ultimately pointing people to Jesus, not to himself.

We all have heroes in our lives: either personal ones who have conducted themselves nobly and lived with great integrity, or more notorious ones who have achieved great things—sometimes despite unbelievably difficult obstacles. However, it is God who gives people their intellect, their courage, their creativity, and their strength. Apart from God, we can achieve nothing (John 15:5), but with God "all things are made possible" (Matt.19:26).

Two modern-day heroes of the faith, whom I mentioned earlier, come to mind. One of them is Bethany Hamilton, who at age thirteen was primed to be one of the youngest great competitive surfers in the world, when she lost her left arm to a shark attack. In the aftermath of the attack, she thought her surfing career was over, even as it was just beginning to take off. She thought she would never be able to surf again. She had found her passion early in life, but it wasn't until the devastating attack took her arm, that she discovered her true calling. She was created to testify to God's greatness and His goodness. She now travels the world sharing her story. She credits God for saving her life and she gives Him all the glory for her ability as a world-class surfer.

---

[98] 1 Tim. 1:15.

Roger Huang grew up as an abused child. In his late teens, he was an angry young man and very insecure. Yet when he came to know the Lord, his heart was set on fire to love and sacrificially serve God by serving the people of the Tenderloin district of San Francisco. His powerful ministry has exploded over the years. This humble man of God has witnessed many mountain-moving miracles in his Christian faith. Even though he is a valiant prayer warrior (fasting and praying are the mainstay of his walk with God), he would tell you that nothing that has been accomplished through him was his own doing. Every victory that has been won was by God's grace and to His glory.

2. *"You shall not make for yourself an idol."* Exodus 20:4

Now more than ever, there are so many things that can be made into an idol. Even the most innocent or useful objects can be made into idols. One of the most common idols is money. God says money in and of itself is not evil. It is the *love of money*—idolizing it, prizing it above Him, that makes it a sinful object. Television can be an idol, if you watch it to the neglect of your relationship with God, your family, or your responsibilities.

I have a friend who by the age of twenty-five was a sports junkie. He literally sat in front of the TV to watch sports all weekend long. He paid no mind to his family, and sadly, as a result, he lost his marriage and, for a period of time, severely damaged his relationship with his children. Mercifully, he found forgiveness from God and has gone on to profoundly influence many lives through sharing his faith and living boldly for the kingdom as a pastor, teacher, coach, mentor, and friend.

Since the advent of high-tech devices such as computers, cell phones, and all kinds of other genius gizmos, our world has enjoyed the convenience, as well as the boundless other benefits derived from all this technology. It has, however, also created a culture where many people are glued to their devices for endless hours, forfeiting meaningful face-to-face interactions and therefore, diminishing the depth of many of their relationships.

It also has made it possible for issues such as cyber-bullying and porn addictions to run rampant. It has been proven that depression is on the rise, in large part, because of some feeling in competition with others. In many cases, isolation and suicide have also increased as a result of social media. The significant increase of distracted drivers has made driving less safe than ever before.

The massive quantity of time spent and the anxiety that comes from any kind of failure in people's technology are indicators that technology is useful only to the extent that it does not become harmful to self or to others. It is the inclination to abuse technology (that which becomes a form of idol worship, not the technology itself) that is sinful.

Don't get me wrong. I see the value of technology and have greatly benefitted from it. However, anything can become an idol if we allow it to be. The enemy is very subtle in his tactics. He uses good and necessary things—like our need for information and communication—and turns them (for some anyway), into addictive and destructive vices. Thankfully, God promises to give us a way of escape when we face temptations of any kind that try to trap us into putting other things ahead of Him. He gives us the antidote in the Great Commandment (Mark 12:30-31). God first, then everyone and everything else comes after that.

A story has often been told of a professor lecturing his class. He pulls out an empty jar and begins filling it with large rocks. Once he places the last rock in the jar, he asks: "Is the jar full?" The students all nod and agree that it is indeed full. Then he starts dropping small pebbles into the jar and shakes the jar periodically to let the pebbles settle toward the bottom. As the jar becomes filled to the top with pebbles, he repeats his question: "Now is the jar full?" Again, the students agree that the jar is full. Then the professor begins to pour sand into the jar. To the students' amazement, they see a once-empty jar filled to the brim with rocks, pebbles, and sand. The point of the story is to not let the minor things in life crowd out the more important things. Had he put the sand and pebbles in the jar first, the big rocks would not all have fit in the jar.

We can easily crowd out God, even by doing good things for Him, or by putting others or ourselves ahead of Him. There seems to always be a constant tension in trying to keep that balance in our lives—not allowing the things of lesser importance to overshadow those which are most important. As my friend with the sports addiction discovered the hard way, when you put God first, you will experience the blessings found in Isaiah 26:3 and Matthew 6:33, but when you don't, you will suffer the consequences.

3. *"You shall not misuse the name of the LORD your God." Exodus 20:7*

Years ago, one of our daughters was helping work with middle-schoolers at church. The topic of discussion on one particular week was about taking the Lord's name in vain. The example she gave the kids was that every time someone says, "Oh, God!" or "Jesus Christ!" or some other phrase that was not intended as a petition meant for God alone, God would immediately reply, "Here I am." The unintentional petitioner would then say, "I wasn't talking to you." The pattern would keep repeating over and over—each time, the person denying any intention of talking to God. Ouch! How entirely disrespectful. These kids were learning about the holiness of God. They were learning what it meant to fear God. Also, about how rude it is to summon someone when you really have no intentions of talking to them at all.

So how would we feel if someone constantly called us by name, then ignored us? I don't imagine anyone would like that much. We all want to be respected and treated with courtesy. Yet we are just mere mortals. Far more does our holy, perfect, and sovereign God deserve our utmost respect. More pointedly, He deserves our reverence, especially when compared to the most prominent people and the highest authorities in our land. No one can hold a candle to our gracious God, our awesome Creator, our loving and compassionate Father.

From a different angle, it is also amazing how many people say that they do not believe in God. Yet when a calamity strikes in their life, their first thought is to say, "Oh, God!" Or they cry out plaintively, "Help me, dear God!" This tendency to call out for God in the midst of despair is due to the innate nature placed within all humans. In Romans 1:20, it says: "For since the creation of the world, God's invisible qualities—his eternal power and divine nature—have been clearly seen, being understood from what has been made, so that men are without excuse."

Somewhere deep inside, we all know there is a Creator. Yet many suppress this knowledge in order to be masters of their own universe. However, when things are out of control in the world or in their personal life, they turn to the only One who is the true Master of the universe. In the aftermath of September 11, churches were filled with people who were searching for solace— searching for answers—searching for hope. When things returned to normal, many of these same people went back to their old ways of profaning the Lord's name without blinking an eye, or only calling out to Him in a moment of need.

God is not a genie that grants wishes. He is not an ER doctor. He is not a credit union loan officer. He created all that is, and is in control of all and all that will be. He knows the number of hairs on each head and the intent of every heart. He has named each star in the sky. He is the Alpha and Omega: the beginning and the end of all things. He loved us enough to sacrifice His sinless Son on the cross to bear all of our sins while we were still His enemies.

When we come to know the one, true God, there is an overwhelming sense of His majesty, His righteousness, and holiness that brings us to our knees in humble adoration and thanksgiving. As believers, we must never lose that sense of God's awesome omniscience, omnipresence, and omnipotence. He knows all. He sees all. He is everywhere. He is all-powerful. Who else can make that claim? Who else is the Great I AM? Who else could we ever love, worship, and serve in this world that deserves such reverence? And one day soon, every knee will bow and every tongue will confess that Jesus Christ is Lord, to the glory of God the Father (see Phil. 2:10-11).

God's name is *powerful.* His great name is able to save, to heal, to forgive, to cleanse, to restore, to bring peace, and to give hope. God's name is *mighty.* It has all authority. It is unique. It is extraordinary. God's name is *holy.* It is the name above all names. It is majestic and mysterious. The Bible is full of illustrations attesting to the majesty of God. In John 14:14, it tells us that if we ask for anything in His name, He will do it. In Acts 4:12 we are told that salvation comes from God alone. Acts 4:30 shows the awesome ability to heal in His holy name—I could go on and on.

For those who have been embraced by the love of God, we have been given every reason to revere His name. For those who have not yet understood the power, the might, and the holiness of God, we must pray for them and authentically live out our faith so that they, too, may also come to love and revere Him.

4. *"Remember the Sabbath day by keeping it holy."*
Exodus 20:8

When I was in Israel eight years ago, I was immediately struck by the devotion and dedication of the Jewish people. Even on the plane heading from New York to Tel Aviv, the orthodox Jewish man, standing in the back corner of our section fascinated me. I tried not to stare at him, but found myself looking up from time to time to watch him perform his daily ritual. After arriving in Tel Aviv, we eventually made our way to Jerusalem. Once there, I observed the earnestness of many devout Jews all around me who clearly loved and feared God. However, it wasn't until we pulled into Tiberius on a Friday evening that I noticed how strictly the commandment to rest from all labor and focus exclusively on God was obeyed.

The town had completely shut down. From sundown to sundown, there were no stores open—no available Laundromat— nowhere to fill up on gas. This was their time of Sabbath rest and absolutely nothing (barring an emergency), would disturb their sacred time with God.

Well, to be honest, it was surprising to me that I was so shocked at this observation. After all, aren't we all meant to take seriously our time for Sabbath rest? Of course, we could easily get sidetracked with the whole issue of what day is the "correct" day to worship God, but let's just set that whole issue aside and focus on the matter at hand.

The reason I was so taken back at how seriously the Jewish people observed the Sabbath was because, in our American culture today, to a large degree, I see how lightly we take this commandment. I will start with my own life. Yes, I worship God in my personal time with Him all through each week. I sing Him songs. I give Him praise. I confess my sins. I sit in silence waiting to hear His voice speaking into my heart and mind. I give Him thanksgiving. I spend many hours studying, memorizing, and meditating on His Word weekly. I also faithfully go to church. All of these are familiar components that are to be practiced by believers—they may not all be practiced every day, by every single believer, but for those who truly walk with the Lord, it is a blessing to faithfully practice these spiritual disciplines.

For some, however, beyond attending worship services, Sabbath rest can be interpreted as "do whatever you please" all day long. Although God certainly does not frown on us spending a large swath of our day to physically "recharge our batteries," I believe by giving us this commandment, He also desires for us to see this as a time to rejuvenate our minds and hearts by reflecting on Him with more intentionality.

Some might argue, "It's my day off. I'm entitled to do what I want," or "I want to have fun. I don't want to sit and read my Bible or pray all day and do nothing else." However, God's command does not say that we cannot have any fun at all on the Sabbath. He takes no pleasure in depriving us of pleasure—quite the opposite. After all, He created us with pleasure in mind. He does, however, expect us to give homage to Him—the very same One who created fun and pleasure.

Although we were created to worship God, it is our joy and privilege—it should not be out of a sense of duty that we do so. It is our humble and grateful response to our holy God and Father. Setting aside time to be with Him and give Him the honor due His name not only glorifies Him, but also benefits us. However, in our busy American culture especially, it is easy to shortchange Him, as well as ourselves. We can easily dilute our quality time with Him, especially on our Sabbath day (whichever day that is for each of us), by letting small "pebbles" and "sand" crowd out precious time with Him.

Went to church—check. Read my Bible—check. Prayed—check. We can easily slip into a more legalistic mindset, if we are not careful. Ticking these things off robotically as part of *our* "to do" list does not please God. What truly honors God is doing these things with a genuine heart of worship. It's not driven by a "have to" attitude, as much as an "I get to" attitude, motivated by love for God.

Another aspect on this matter is with regard to working on the Sabbath. God clearly desires people to avoid working on the Sabbath as much as possible. However, in some situations, it is unavoidable. For instance, when labor has to be performed. After all, our need of certain services demands workers in 24-7 jobs such as hospital workers, policemen, firemen, and many other critical occupations. In some situations, economic hardship requires someone to take a job where they must work on Sundays, if it's the only way to provide for their family. As Jesus addresses this issue of working on the Sabbath with the Pharisees in Mark 2:27-28, He is showing that it is the spirit of the law and not the letter of the law that truly matters.

As we may apply it to non-essential labor on the Sabbath, such as doing chores, going grocery shopping, and so forth, it is preferable to arrange our schedules to not do these things, if possible. However, in some occupations (take farmers, for instance), they may be obligated to perform certain chores on the Sabbath. A fair number of people have legitimate reasons to do some form of labor on the Lord's Day of rest. None of these things are bad things to do. In fact, they are often necessary tasks. However, if we have designated a certain day of the week to be our Sabbath day, then the goal is to fulfill as many of our obligations on other days and set aside this one day for the Lord, to the greatest extent and with the best intent possible.

This is a goal I have yet to fully attain. I don't always get it right. Some weeks are better than others. Sometimes, I make poor choices and slip into "Martha mode" instead of "Mary mode" (Luke 10:39-42). I slacked the day before—getting detoured by some project and so I didn't get to the store to buy what's needed for Sunday evening's dinner. I did chores that could have been done on another day. My sleep schedule was disrupted and as a result, I rushed through a very abbreviated amount of time with the Lord before church, while spending a great deal of time afterwards "puttering" on a ministry project.

For the most part, since my time in Israel, I have become more keenly aware of my actions and activities on the Sabbath day. I try not to merely "chill out," but to put a more concentrated effort into my time with God on these days. It might be pondering an application from the morning sermon. It might be more extensive time in prayer. It might be going for a walk or taking a drive to take in the wonder of His creation. It might be spending time with family. Also (as much as possible), it involves fasting from my technology.

Whatever our Sabbath day looks like for each one of us, it's never meant to be legalistic, boring, or methodical. It is intended to be restful, replenishing, and above all, worshipful.

5. *"Honor your father and your mother." Exodus 20:12*

Growing up in Northern California in the 60's and 70's, my parents did a good job of raising my siblings and I to show respect to them and to our elders, in general. They did not just teach us good manners, but also a deeply held respect for those who were in authority over us. However, as in every family, there were times when my siblings and I disobeyed our parents in various ways: by slacking on our chores, talking back to them, provoking our siblings in some way, and so forth.

Just as it is innate in our nature to know that there is a Creator, it is also innate in our fleshly nature to sin, even against those we love and respect. Still, it is hard for many people to fathom how an infant born into this world could be a sinner. After all, they haven't actually committed any sins yet and they are completely helpless. Yet God tells us that, "*all* have sinned and fall short of the glory of God" (Rom. 3:23—*emphasis mine*).

Now we could embark on a whole theological debate on this issue, but the point of my bringing this up is that as the infant becomes a toddler, it does not take long to see their sinful nature manifested. It is in this early stage of life that they begin to test the boundaries their parents have imposed on them for their own protection and development. It is also the time when they begin to learn about what is appropriate behavior and what is not, in order to grow up and responsibly relate to the world around them.

By the time a child enters their teen years, they have begun to more clearly formulate and assert their own views on what is acceptable behavior with others. In a number of cases, they might even entirely cast off restraint and actually show a disdain for the foundation of respect and protocol taught by their parents. By the time they reach adulthood, they have either decided to remain in keeping with the foundation of their early years, have adopted some new form of it, or have launched out into a whole new value system that vaguely or in no way resembles the former one.

As we apply these phases of child development to the Fifth Commandment, we will now move from a general evaluation to a more specific focus within the realm of Christian families and how it relates to our current cultural climate. In generations past, an important part of raising children was taking them to church and teaching them to obey their parents (along with all the other commandments). Although church was very much a part of family life back then, Christian education primarily took place at home. However, since 1962, when the Supreme Court ruled to ban prayer from public schools and our country began to move away from the Bible, we have witnessed the profound ramifications of this departure away from God as the central authority for people.[99]

Over the many years since, we have seen not only a significant diminishing of courtesy and respect for others, in general, but we have also witnessed the assault on the family unit. The results have been devastating. A number of factors have contributed to this change, in addition to what I have already cited: (1) Households have gone from one to predominantly two-income families; (2) Many couples now commonly practice role-reversal; (3) Divorce became lawful for reasons other than abandonment. These changes have ushered in an increase in cases of divorce, abuse, addiction, gang participation and more.

When God instructed Adam and Eve to procreate, it was in order to offer reconciliation to a desperately

---

[99] Engel v. Vitale

broken world. After their fall from grace, Eve conceived and gave birth to Cain. She later gave birth to Abel. The "new normal" on earth was nothing like Paradise. How quickly things moved from a perfect world, where all was at peace (Gen. 1:28), to a world where pain and death became a part of life (Gen. 3-4:8).

Fast-forwarding on through Jacob and Esau, Ishmael and Isaac, Joseph and his brothers, we can see how sin tainted family dynamics and often brought grief and shame upon the parents. Of course, at times, the parents helped cause the strife, but you would have to say that sin was at the root of it all.

Knowing what we know about sin and how it wreaks havoc in relationships between parents and children, what positive biblical examples of children obeying their parents can we soundly observe? Well, Isaac, for one, as he follows his father Abraham, up to Mount Moriah. As they begin their trek up the mountain, he doesn't know that his father is about to face a severe test of his faith. Even though it's never mentioned in the Bible, Isaac was facing his own test of obedience as his father was preparing him to be sacrificed. Although the Bible does not specify his age, several clues make it probable that he was at least a teen at the time.[100]

He could have resisted his father. He could have argued with him. We do know that he did not run away. He allowed his father to build the altar, preparing him to be the sacrificial offering. Abraham was acting in obedience to His Father. Isaac, in his way, was also obeying his father. For us, the notion of putting our own child on an altar is an abhorrent thought, yet,

---

[100]Gen. 22: 7-8.

what an extraordinary picture of obedience we have been given in this passage!

Of course, the most perfect example we have in God's Word is of Jesus Himself. In Luke 2:41-50, we come upon this scene of Jesus and His earthly parents going to the temple for the annual feast at Passover. He was only twelve years old at the time, yet He already had grown "strong" and was "filled with wisdom" (Luke 2:40).

In the next frame, we see Him in the temple interacting with the learned men who were there. Meanwhile, His parents had begun to travel back home until they discovered that Jesus was not among those in their caravan. When they returned to Jerusalem to look for Him, they found Him in the temple. When Mary confronts her son and asks why He has caused their anxiety, He replies, "Didn't you know I had to be in my Father's house?" (v. 48).

Okay, so you might say, "Uh, well, maybe this isn't such a perfect example of obedience after all!" For one thing, wasn't He disobeying them by not getting their permission to go to the temple? You might also maintain that Jesus was a special case. He wasn't just anyone's son. He was the Son of God. However, He was also the Son of Man. He was fully human. He had earthly parents, as well as His Father in heaven. Given the situation at hand, He was compelled to obey His heavenly Father. He was exactly where He needed to be. Also, we do see Him honoring His earthly parents in verses 51-52: "Then he went down to Nazareth with them and was obedient to them. But his mother treasured all these things in her heart. And Jesus grew in wisdom and stature, and in favor with God and men."

Of course, the ultimate example God gave us was that of His Son yielding to the Father, as we see in the account of the Garden of Gethsemane—Matt. 26:42. Further, we observe it as He completes His earthly mission on the cross (John 19:30). Despite the overwhelming grief He felt at Gethsemane over the gravity of what He was about to endure, He willingly submitted to His Father in obedience to Him.

On the cross, He honored His heavenly Father by crying out to Him in the midst of His suffering (Mark 15:34); praying for forgiveness for His enemies (Luke 23:34); showing mercy to one of the two thieves on the cross (Luke 23:43); showing concern for His mother and one of His disciples (John 19:26-27); and finally, completing the mission His Father had given Him (John 19:30).

At times, our challenge to honor God (as well as our earthly parents) is made so unnecessarily more painful and complicated than need be as we wrestle with our rebellious flesh nature. Of course, there are also times when it is difficult, if not impossible, to do so. For instance, in the case of an extremely abusive or dangerous parent, when the child (even though perhaps now an adult), may need to distance themself and can honor them only by praying for them and seeking to forgive them.

Overall, however, the way to honor our parents is simply to obey them. To show them love and respect. To not provoke them or do anything that would bring shame on them. When we honor our parents, we are honoring God. And in circular fashion, by our loving God, we learn well how to love and honor our parents.

1. List some things that can be considered idols. Examine your own life and ask God to bring to your awareness anything that might be an idol to you. Confess it as sin and ask Him for forgiveness.

2. Think about how you spend time on your Sabbath day. Do you feel that you set aside a God-pleasing amount of time to worship, reflect, and be rejuvenated? If you believe there's room for improvement, consider how you might increase the quality of your time with Him. Then, make a commitment and follow through.

3. List some ways we can honor our parents. What are the benefits of fulfilling this commandment (see Proverbs 1:8-9 and 10:1)?

CHAPTER 25

LAW

The Ten Commandments: Part Two
Exodus 20:13-17

6. *"You shall not commit murder." Exodus 20:13*

For most believers, it is a no-brainer that we will never commit murder or have any inclination toward committing any kind of violent act. Yet there are believers who have taken a life in crimes of passion, through poor and reckless choices (such as a DUI or distracted driving, leading to vehicular manslaughter), or through abortion, euthanasia, or suicide. This by no means covers all the reasons it happens, but tragically, it does happen.

For the past sixteen years, my husband has been the chaplain county jail and juvenile hall, and in addition, has founded a nationwide prison ministry.[101] Believe me, he has encountered many believers in the jail and prison system. What has been made clear to

---

[101] *www.targettruthministries.com*

him over the years, as he meets with inmates at our local jail or corresponds with prisoners by mail, is that not every person who is incarcerated is evil. In fact, a great many of the people who end up in jail or prison are not evil people, they are just lost people who have made some really bad choices—often resulting in very serious consequences.

That said, it is easy to think that this commandment only addresses "those" people and applies only to the taking of another's life. However, the Sixth Commandment encompasses so much more than that. Sin has infected and thus, has affected us all. Our sinful nature creates all kinds of opportunities for us to be tempted and even commit various types of murder. It is to this end, that we will explore this commandment in depth.

In the story of David and Bathsheba (2 Sam. 11-12), it is easy to focus on David's sin of having Bathsheba's husband Uriah killed. Although at the root of the story is the lust he had for Bathsheba, which led to him committing adultery, which in turn led to Uriah's death. God's Word tells us in James 1:14-15 that "each one is tempted when, by his own evil desire, he is dragged away and enticed. Then, after desire has conceived, it gives birth to sin, and sin, when it is full-grown, gives birth to death."

Even though David was "a man after God's own heart" (Acts 13:22), he, along with every other human being who ever walked the earth, with the exception of Jesus, was susceptible to the enemy's schemes and the feebleness of his own fallen nature. Jeremiah 17:9 tells us, "the heart is deceitful above all things and beyond cure." The good news is that although none of us can fully prevent temptation, Jesus will always provide a way out (1 Cor. 10:13). By laying down our carnal lives, our strong wills, our fleshly desires, and leaving them at the foot of the cross, we are set free from the bondage that leads to death.

We are told in God's Word that it doesn't even have to involve committing an actual act (such as adultery), for it to be considered a sin in God's eyes. Matthew 5:28 cautions us, "anyone who looks at a woman lustfully has already committed adultery with her in his heart."

In the case of David, however, he followed through with the act of adultery, which led to Bathsheba conceiving his child. The domino effect of his sinful actions eventually led to the death of the child he conceived with Bathsheba, among other repercussions.

Another area that is considered a form of murder is the character assassination of another person. When we slander, gossip, or bully someone (instead of speaking kindly of or to others), we are damaging and in many cases, destroying their reputation. In this age of social media, we are seeing some extreme effects of character assassination. Many people (including vulnerable children and youth) are taking their own lives as a result of malicious slanders, gossip, and cyber-bullying. Yet God exhorts us in 1 Peter 2:1 to, "rid [our]selves of all malice and all deceit, hypocrisy, envy and slander of every kind."

If we have a difference of opinion, an argument, or have been offended in some way by someone, we are to pray for them and seek to give a right response to them. The answer is to not involve others who have no part in the dispute, but instead, to apply the Golden Rule (Luke 6:31; Matt. 7:12). We are also not to divulge someone's secret, spoken to us in confidence (Prov. 25:9). Bearing false witness impugns and can actually destroy a person's character. However, we will examine this more closely under the Ninth Commandment.

Abortion

One of the hot-button issues of our day is the topic of abortion. Many people believe that they can make a strong defense for taking the life of an unborn baby. First of all, at the core of the pro-choice argument is that it's a woman's right to do whatever she wants with her own body. Secondly, that the fetus is merely "a clump of cells" and is not a human being until it is born (or up to a certain point after it is born).

This is such a highly sensitive and hugely controversial topic and cannot be given its due diligence in a book such as this. However, it is important to give it some well-deserved attention, as it speaks directly to what is deemed murder in the eyes of the Lord.

On the matter of ownership of the body, one of the verses that speaks most clearly on this topic, is found in 1 Corinthians 6:19-20:

> *Do you not know that your body is a temple of the Holy Spirit, who is in you, whom you have received from God? You are not your own; you were bought at a price. Therefore honor God with your body* (See also Rom. 12:1; 1 Cor. 3:16).

For those who do not know and revere the Lord, it is easy to disregard God's commandment and insist upon a woman's right to choose. And for some believers (especially those facing an unplanned or unwanted pregnancy), aborting a child can seem like the only way out, and therefore, can be justified. They may reason: "If God is a God of forgiveness, He will forgive me." Yes, indeed, God does forgive those who repent of sin and seek His forgiveness. The problem is that there are still consequences to violating His laws. Oftentimes, the most severe consequence of all is the inability to forgive oneself after an abortion.

As to the matter of a fetus only being "a clump of cells" and not a real person, Jeremiah 1:5 clearly refutes this claim saying, "Before I formed you in the womb I knew you, before you were born I set you apart." Further, David emphatically exclaims in Psalm 139:13-16:

> *For you created my inmost being; you knit me together in my mother's womb. I praise you because I am fearfully and wonderfully made; your works are wonderful, I know that full well. My frame was not hidden from you when I was made in the secret place. When I was woven together in the depths of the earth, your eyes saw my unformed body. All the days ordained for me were written in your book before one of them came to be.*

Euthanasia and Suicide

As with the issue of abortion, euthanasia and suicide are issues that cannot be fully addressed in this book, but cannot be entirely overlooked either. These are both very serious issues with severe earthly and eternal ramifications.

Driven by a growing trend toward self-rule, situational ethics, and an increasing pulling away from God's absolute truth and holy standards, we see many ethical, political, and religious debates occurring in our society today. They are often volatile and irreconcilable.

As long as people move away from God's laws, they will be at odds with the divine order. Trying to remove God's authority from our lives not only affects the quality of our lives, but also the outcome of our lives. It also affects the lives of others as well.

In the case of euthanasia, many try to justify the killing of someone who is in a desperate state as an act of mercy. But what may seem like a compassionate act to some, is believed to be a criminal act to others. More importantly, though, it is an affront to God Almighty.

First of all, God's Word informs us that He and He alone is the Giver of life (Gen. 1:27, 2:7). Secondly, He is the only one who should decide when a life ends. In the book of Job we read that, "Man's days are determined; you have decreed the number of his months and have set limits he cannot exceed" (14:5). We are further assured of this truth in Psalm 139:

> *All the days ordained for me were written*
> *in your book before one of them came to*
> *be. (v. 16)*

Even with the best of intentions, it is never our place to play God as it pertains to euthanasia or suicide (or in any other case, for that matter). That is exactly what has gotten us in trouble from the very beginning of time.

In both cases, there are also lesser considerations to take into account. In an article entitled, *What About the Terminally Ill?* it is reported: "a study of terminally ill patients published in The American Journal of Psychiatry in 1986 concluded, 'Most terminal patients seek suicide not because they are ill, but because they are depressed.' "[102]

Further, in a separate article by Balch and David Walters, they maintain that:

> Proponents of euthanasia argue that "mercy killing" is necessary because patients, particularly those with terminal illness, experience uncontrollable pain. They argue that the only way to alleviate the pain is to eliminate the patient.[103]

Doctors, nurses, and other medical professionals are in the business of saving lives. Their role should never be to deliberately take a life. By doing so, they are presumptuously and erroneously assuming the authority of God. God has sovereignty over all. Those who try to usurp His authority will pay a severe penalty in the end (Deut. 32:35).

There is nothing wrong with being merciful. God expects compassion and mercy from us. But as with just about anything else on earth (if carried to an extreme), these attributes can actually be harmful,

---

[102]Burke J. Balch, J.D., and Randall K. O' Bannon, M.A., *Why We Shouldn't Legalize Assisting Suicide: Part III: What About the Terminally Ill?* (www.nrlc. org/medethics/directkilling, 1-11-13).

[103]Burke J Balch, J.D., and David Walters, *Why We Shouldn't Legalize Assisting Suicide: Part II: Pain Control* (www.nrlc.org/medethics/directkilling, 1-1-13).

dangerous, or disastrous. Once we slide down the slippery slope of self-rule, instead of submitting to God's authority and following His rules, we set ourselves up for His wrath. Meanwhile, others suffer loss prematurely or deny their loved ones precious time with them.

7. *"You shall not commit adultery." Exodus 20:14*

Let's face it, we are now living not only in an age where adultery is tolerated and even commonplace, but also in an age where the institution of marriage is under severe assault. As we reflect on the Sixth Commandment, it is equally important for us to examine God's intended design for marriage, as it is to look at the appeal and effects of adultery.

The obvious biblical example that comes to mind is David's relationship with Bathsheba. Certainly no discussion on adultery from a biblical worldview is complete without this story. We will look at this in greater detail momentarily. However, adultery runs rampant all through the Bible as we read of multiple marriages, concubines, affairs, orgies, homosexuality, and fornication with prostitutes.

In modern times, we know that bigamy, affairs, and prostitution still exist, along with other sexual immorality such as: pornography, pedophilia, bestiality, and sex trafficking. So what do these all have in common? Many would say, "Well, that's obvious...sex." While true, sex is the physical manifestation of adultery in its varying forms, the thread that ties them all together is a spiritual perversion of God's plan for expressing intimacy exclusively between a man and a woman in marriage. It can come from lust, pride, weakness, greed, discontentment, a need to control, insecurity, or in some cases, just pure evil.

We know that great men of God like Joseph, David, and Solomon were not exempt from facing temptation of one kind or another. In the case of Joseph, he held strong in resisting the advances made by Potiphar's wife. David, though he committed sins along the way (both with Bathsheba and in taking on multiple wives), was still "a man after God's own heart." Solomon, on the other hand, though he began as a wise and godly man, traded in his blessings for burdens as he sought to feed his fleshly desires, time and time again.

Of course, we can't just pick on the men. Many women also willingly committed adulterous acts, as is noted about the background of Rahab (Josh. 2), Gomer (Hosea chapters 1 and 3), the sinful woman who anointed Jesus' feet with perfume (Luke 7), the unnamed woman at the well (John 4), and the woman who wasn't stoned (John 8). However, the profound message we can glean through the portraits of David and these women in particular, is that God redeems sinful people and purifies them so that they may glorify Him. He is a holy God and He demands holiness from His people—whether single or married.

God's intended design for marriage was that it be between one man and one woman (1 Cor. 7:1-2; 1 Tim. 3:2), and that it be a relationship in which each spouse respects and cherishes the other. Its purpose is three-fold: (1) For procreation; (2) for companionship; and (3) to illustrate what the Body of Christ should look like as the Bride of Christ (Eph. 5:22-33).

Although Genesis 2:18 tells us that God created woman to be a companion for man (because "it was not

good for the man to be alone"), it is not entirely in con-
tradiction with 1 Corinthians 7:1 which states: "It is
good for a man not to marry." In his letter to the church
at Corinth, Paul was trying to convey that a single man
is better able to focus solely on God. Whereas, in the
case of a married man, he has to divide his attention
between God and his wife—his love for God may be
deep, but his time and energy are more limited by his
giving affection to his spouse.

Here, Paul is obviously not recommending that
everyone should stay single, for he goes on to say, "But
since there is so much immorality, each man should
have his own wife, and each woman her own husband"
(see also vv. 8-9). His point is that if one can stay single,
that is preferable. If they cannot control their physical
desires, then it is better to be married.

God created us for relationship. He first and foremost wants us to be in relationship with Him. He
also wants us to be in relationship with one another.
However, the intimacy found between a husband and
wife in a marriage relationship is a uniquely holy union.
That is why at a wedding, when a couple is reciting
their vows to one another, they are making a covenant
with each other before God and witnesses that they will
love each other purely and exclusively.

As we revisit David's relationship with Bathsheba,
we see both the appeal this adulterous affair had to
him, and then the long-range effects it had on his marriage and family.

Delving further into this tragic failing in David's life,
we discover that there was a three-strike digression that,
for a period in time, took David from his esteemed role
as a warrior-king to a loathsome adulterer-murderer.

As the story unfolds, David uncharacteristically stays back in Jerusalem as his army goes off to war to fight the Ammonites. Had he stuck with his usual modus operendi, he might never have ended up in the hot mess he created for himself and for others. But for whatever reason, he remained in Jerusalem where he got caught in the tempter's snare.

As he took a walk one night on his roof, he caught sight of a beautiful woman bathing. *Strike 1—Lust*: He asked one of his palace staff to inquire about who she was and then had her brought to him. *Strike 2— Deceit*: He slept with Bathsheba and she became pregnant. He then panicked and sought to hide his sin with yet another sin: by having her husband Uriah summoned home so that Uriah would sleep with his wife, the pregnancy would be explainable. However, his plan backfired when Uriah refused David's suggestion that he take some leave time and remain in Jerusalem. The honorable Uriah could not, in all good conscience, allow his men to be in harm's way while he stayed in comfort and safety at home for an extended period.

David then proceeded to get him drunk in hopes he would go home and sleep with his wife. However, his plan failed again. *Strike 3—Desperation*: At this point, David felt he had no other recourse but to send Uriah back to the frontlines and order that he be strategically placed where he was sure to be killed. This time his plan succeeded, but his "success" was redefined from that point on as it led to severe, ongoing consequences in his life.

Despite David's transgression and resulting turmoil, God has seen fit to make use of his story to give us a substantial warning of the lure of lust and the painful reality of immorality. David's marriage continued on, but not without suffering some permanent damage. As mentioned earlier in this chapter, the child conceived through his adultery with Bathsheba died. His legacy was further tarnished by the events that would follow: his son Ammon raping his sister Tamar, his son Absalom killing Ammon for defiling Tamar, Absalom trying to overthrow his father as king, David fleeing in fear of his own son, Absalom's death, and on it went. It has all the makings of a classic Shakespearean play. And yet, sadly, it is a true story of a great king whose disobedience led to much needless heartache.

Had he remained in God's perfect will, obeying God rather than giving into temptation, his life and legacy would have looked much different.

It is very easy for us as humans to give into our flesh nature. However, no matter how difficult it may be to resist our flesh and the enemy's temptations, it is well worth the effort, in order to avoid painful consequences and have peace with God. We have also been assured as we combat temptation that He will always provide a way of escape (1 Cor. 10:13).

8. *"You shall not steal." Exodus 20:15*

It is a pretty safe bet that when most people think of the Eighth Commandment, their minds easily conjure up an image of someone robbing a person or business of their money or other possessions. Yet there are a myriad of other forms of stealing.

In this high-tech society that we live in, all kinds of piracy occurs as artists, musicians, inventors, and writers fall readily prey to having their creative work ripped off. Hackers steal people's personal account information (or worse, their identity), and it can entirely ruin their lives. There are all kinds of scams: on the phone, by mail, or online. There are embezzlers, tax frauds, and tax evaders. Corporations steal from each other. Countries spy and steal national secrets from one another.

Still, there are many forms of robbery that we might be tempted to regard as "lesser forms:" Cheating on a test, being undercharged at the store and not correcting the error, failing to return a borrowed item, not tipping for good service, not giving an employer an honest days' work for an honest day's wages—on and on it goes. Yet the truth of the matter is, stealing is stealing—no matter what form it takes or what degree of damage it causes.

In the case of cheating, you might say that cheating is not stealing (dishonest, yes), but not stealing. The *American Heritage Dictionary* (Second College Edition) defines the word "dishonest" as: "Disposed to lie, cheat, defraud or deceive." However, say if someone gets away with cheating on a test and is rewarded with a scholarship, a job, or some other undeserved status or position, they are robbing another person of what is rightfully theirs.

As Christians, we have a responsibility to represent the name of Jesus Christ with the utmost honesty and integrity. When we fail to correct the error at the grocery store, when we fail to return a book to a friend, when we don't tip our server equitably (or at all) at a restaurant, or give less than our best effort at our job, we are a poor witness to others and an affront to God.

Dishonesty and stealing go hand in hand and God detests them both equally. In Matthew 21:12-13, we see a rare moment in Jesus' ministry where He displays outright anger toward the moneychangers in the temple. They are pretending to be righteous in their actions and yet are taking advantage of the poor, while at the same time, robbing the temple of its due tithes. Jesus showed His disdain for their greed and for their shameless lack of reverence as He called them out on the carpet: "'It is written,' he said to them, 'My house will be called a house of prayer,' but you are making it a 'den of robbers'" (v. 13).

In the story of Ananias and Sapphira (Acts 5:1-11), we read of how they robbed God by selling a piece of property and withholding some of the profit for themselves, rather than tithing it to the church. The result? Just as sharply as Peter addressed this serious offense and unforced error, God's wrath came down upon Ananias and he perished. Sapphira, also confronted by Peter about this travesty, unashamedly denied her sin and met the same bitter end.

Malachi chapter 3 paints a crystal clear picture of both God's righteousness and His graciousness:

> *I the LORD do not change. So you, O*
> *descendants of Jacob, are not destroyed.*
> *Ever since the time of your forefathers you*
> *have turned away from my decrees and*
> *have not kept them. Return to me, and I will*
> *return to you," says the LORD Almighty.*
>
> *"But you ask, 'How are we to return?*
> *"Will a man rob God? Yet you rob me.*

"But you ask, 'How do we rob you?'

*"In tithes and offerings. You are under a
curse—the whole nation of you—because
you are robbing me. Bring the whole tithe
into the storehouse, that there may be food
in my house. Test me in this," says the
LORD Almighty, "and see if I will not throw
open the floodgates of heaven and pour out
so much blessing that you will not have
room enough for it." (vv. 6-10)*

God longs to bless those whose hearts are fully His.
Yet the natural tendency of man leans toward self-ful-
fillment ahead of pleasing God. That's what got Adam
and Eve in trouble—and Jacob—and the rich young
ruler—and it can also trip us up, too, if we allow our
priorities to go awry. Ironically, the very desire to please
self first is that which robs a person of the fullness of
God's rich blessings:

*Honor the Lord with your wealth, with
the firstfruits of all your crops; then your
barns will be filled to overflowing, and
your vats will brim over with new wine.*
Proverbs 3:9-10

God intends for us to enjoy His abundant riches
now—not only when we get to heaven. How much it
must sadden our Abba Father's heart to want to give
to us, His precious children, "every spiritual blessing"
(Eph. 1:3). And yet, we can so easily miss out on some

of these blessings because we withhold from Him a portion of that which already belongs to Him.

I'm not just referring purely to financial resources either. It can just as easily apply to our time, talents, and spiritual gifts as well. We can be "holy hoarders" (as was the man in the parable of the talents—see Matt. 25), and pay the penalty for it.

Our enemy, the most clever and cunning thief of all, comes to "steal, kill and destroy,"[104] as he continually tries to tempt us to hold back from God or trick us out of the good things God has for us. Truthfully, however, the blame does not fall squarely on him. We have been given the gift of free will and with it comes the responsibility to be good stewards of all God has entrusted to us and to give back to God that which belongs to Him.

He gave us our various spiritual gifts in order for us to build up the Body of Christ and to help grow the kingdom of God. He expects us to use our gifts effectively and generously. Our freedom in Christ gives us an ongoing opportunity to express our praise and gratitude to God, as well as to share with others the hope we have in Jesus.

When we fail to set aside time with Him, we are depriving ourselves of the privilege of knowing Him better and discerning His will for our lives more clearly. We are also robbing Him of the joy of being with us. When we withhold using our talents and spiritual gifts (due to wrong priorities, stubbornness, self-doubt, or laziness), we are devaluing God's investment by limiting the potential to bear fruit (John 15:5, 16).

---

[104]John 10:10.

Finally, in addition to the assorted forms of high-tech robbery mentioned before, we can steal other people's sense of security or peace of mind when our pride trumps their reasonable sense of well-being in any way.

Arsonists cause the loss of homes, property, and loss of life—robbing them of their security, livelihood, and loved ones. Drug dealers hook others into an endless cycle of addiction—destroying dreams, minds, and lives. And, in ever-increasing numbers, perpetrators force victims into various forms of slavery—stealing their: (1) right to privacy (and in many cases their innocence), (2) their sense of self-worth so that their lives are deprived of freedom to choose where and how they live, and (3) their right to live free of fear. Though any form of stealing is reprehensible in God's eyes, I believe that this particular form of stealing must be at the top of the list of that which is most abhorrent to Him.

The Israelites had a lot of experience with slavery. Their time in Egypt and in captivity to the Assyrians and the Babylonians was a painful lesson in the wretchedness of the human condition. Although slavery was common back in biblical times, it was never a part of God's original plan for man. God shows us throughout His Word that stealing (in any form) is not only wrong, but brings serious consequences. His heart of justice seeks to protect victims and punish anyone who takes that which does not belong to them.

9. *"You shall not give false testimony against your neighbor." Exodus 20:16*

There are all kinds of reasons that people bear false testimony: guilt, pride, jealousy, greed, ambition, bitterness, revenge, political agendas, and more. When a person makes a false statement about another, they are not only damaging that person's reputation, they are also sentencing themselves to severe judgment.

The Bible gives us numerous examples of someone bearing false witness against another. Some of the well-known passages we can look to are: Potiphar's wife against Joseph (Gen. 39:7-20), Herod to the Magi (Matt. 2:7-9), the Jews against Paul (Acts 24-25), and most notably, the chief priests against Jesus (Matt. 26:57-68).

In the case of Potiphar's wife, she lusted after Joseph and tried to seduce him. However, Joseph, being a godly man, full of honor and integrity, would not succumb to temptation and refused her advances. So when her husband returned home, the spurned woman falsely accused Joseph of attempting to violate her. Consequently, Potiphar had him thrown in jail.

Though the Bible speaks no further of Potiphar's wife, we can be sure that her sin of bearing false witness would ultimately be adjudicated in God's high court. Joseph, on the other hand (though innocent of the charges), humbly accepted the punishment and received God's favor as a result (v. 21).

After Jesus was born, the Magi sought to find the Christ Child so that they could bring Him gifts and worship Him. When they inquired of King Herod as to where they might find the child, he felt threatened and so he responded to their inquiry with deception—saying that he, too, wanted to worship the newborn king.

However, after they found the Child, the Magi were warned in a dream not to return to Herod. So they returned to their native lands and did not report back to him. In this story (just as in the previous one), it is a fair assumption that God's justice would eventually prevail, even if at the time of the event, it may seem that the transgressor got away with their sin.

In Acts 24-25, we learn of a large contingent of co-conspirators (high-ranking men such as Ananias the high priest, Tertullus the attorney, elders, as well as common Jews from Jerusalem), who set off a chain of judicial events, adding to the cast of characters (Festus the governor of Judea, King Agrippa and Caesar), that eventually led to Paul's house arrest in Rome.

Paul was being accused of "[stirring] up dissension among the Jews" and being "a ringleader of the sect of the Nazarenes" (Acts 24:5 NASB). Acts 25:7 confirms that these serious charges were presented with no evidence to corroborate them.

God clearly warns us in Proverbs 6:16-19 of the Seven Deadly Sins—one of which is bearing false witness against another (v. 19). Before we point the finger at others and say, "How could that person say such a thing?" or "Look at them. They are such a gossip," we should stop and first examine our own lives, to make sure that our own speech in no way impugns the reputation of another.

I know that in my life, at times I have made statements based on assumptions, with no hard facts to back them up. I have also in a moment of hurt, anger, or frustration lashed out and said a harsh or unflattering word that might cause a bystander to think less of another person. Behaviors such as this may be explainable and forgivable, but they are never excusable.

The book of James offers much instruction to us on the taming of the tongue. In chapter 3, we are told that: (1) the tongue is capable of setting a metaphorical forest fire (v. 5); (2) "no one can tame the tongue; it is a restless evil and full of deadly poison" (v. 8); and (3) "if you have bitter jealousy and selfish ambition in your heart, do not be arrogant and so lie against the truth...[for it] is earthly...[and in it] there is disorder and every evil thing" (vv. 14-16).

Further, Ephesians 4:31-32 admonishes us to, "put away slander" and rather, "be kind to one another,... forgiving...just as God in Christ also has forgiven you." When Jesus was brought in a cloak of darkness to the Sanhedrin in a sham trial, He faced false allegations and His determined accusers with the same wisdom, humility, and restraint we had seen Him display all throughout His public ministry.

Even as He hung on the cross, with people hurling insults, and directing vile, slanderous remarks at Him, He exclaimed, "Father, forgive them, for they do not know what they are doing" (Luke 23:34). And yet, even knowing the devastating effect a false witness against another can bring, we can still be tempted to inflict deliberate harm on another by misrepresenting them or slanting the truth of a situation for selfish gain. We can be hasty in our assessment of people and situations and (in our ignorance or arrogance), want to weigh in with our opinion, rather than facts. If only we would choose to always view people from God's perspective and seek to build them up rather than find reasons to tear them down.

10. *"You shall not covet your neighbor's house."*

Exodus 20:17

In chapter 9, I mentioned a dubious band of brothers: Cain and Abel, Jacob and Esau, Joseph and his brothers—each of whom were at odds with one another. In each case of conflict between the brothers, you could easily explain it away as, "Well, that's just what brothers do...they fight. They can't help it. Blame it on testosterone or maybe you might be tempted to say that these men (like so many others) had a competitive spirit...no mystery there.

However, in the case of the above examples (as with numerous modern-day situations), the heart of the matter usually stems from pride, pure and simple. Whereas, anger, resentment, and hatred are *results* of pride, covetousness (jealousy or envy) is a *form* of pride and often is found to be the culprit in a battle of the wills. Now it would be wildly erroneous to broad-brush and say that all fighting is due to coveting something or someone. But even though it is not the sole reason, in many cases, this is the prevailing cause and effect.

I believe that when it comes to people, generally speaking, we all long to be guaranteed a reasonable standard of living. However, in particular, there has always been a tension between the "haves" and the "have not's." Some "with means" have raised the tension by brazenly flaunting their wealth. They live by the words of the familiar bumper sticker: "Whoever dies with the most toys, wins." On the opposite end of the spectrum, many of those trying to "keep up with the Joneses" spend their whole lives trapped in a quagmire of unfulfilled longings, resulting in disappointment, despair, and defeat. It is not a fair competition and there are no true winners.

Let's face it—we live in a consumer-crazed society. This is not necessarily a new concept—it's just that the "toys" get faster, cooler, and costlier. I'm always amazed during the holidays when I hear news segments about people who stay up well into the night to catch the "Black Friday" specials—or the ones who pitch tents and sleep for several days outside in the wet, cold elements just to be one of the first in a long line to get the latest iPhone or other hot, new item.

A spirit of discontentment brings dishonor to God and no real peace of mind to our lives. God intended for us to rest in Him and trust His provision for our needs, as well as for our deepest desires. He wants us to value the things He values: love, humility, integrity, justice, mercy, and peace. It gives Him no pleasure to watch His beloved creation stress or obsess over "getting ahead," acquiring "the most," and worrying to the point of experiencing high blood pressure, depression, or other stress-induced maladies.

Years ago, while visiting an affluent town in the Bay Area for the day, I became enamored by the beautiful homes in this charming community. Some homes were mansions and some were just older, middle-class homes, yet homes with a lot of character and curb appeal. As the day wore on, I found myself feeling more and more unsettled as a spirit of envy crept in. I remember trying to picture myself living in one of those homes, even knowing the possibility of owning one of them was not at all realistic.

When we finally arrived back home that evening, we found a note on our front door from our neighbor saying, "Come see us about the fire." We tore through our house looking for any evidence of a fire, yet found none. We then went out to investigate our backyard and found extensive damage there.

We came to find out that earlier in the day, the neighbor kids next door were playing with matches in the toolshed that butted up to our shared fence. In a very short time, things were out of control and not only did their shed and the fence catch fire, but the branches from the trees at our fence line also went up in flames and were raining burning embers into our yard.

Had it not been for the quick response from our neighbors hosing down things down until the fire department arrived, we would have lost our home. We so appreciated them for not hesitating to take action. We were very thankful that the children involved were not harmed. And, naturally, we were beyond grateful we still had a home. Our sweet home, where so many memories had been made. Our home we had fixed up to suit our style and comfort. Our home where love filled the air and our hearts.

It was more than just a roof over our heads. It was a precious and extravagant gift from God that, for a moment in time, I had taken for granted. The lessons from that day were profound and lasting. I was humbled to the core as, in my longing for something I was not meant to have, I lost sight of what I already did have and almost lost.

In Matthew 6:25-34 and Philippians 4:19, He makes it abundantly clear that He is not only our *soul Provider*, but that He is our *sole Provider*. He admonishes us not to worry, and yet we do (Luke 12:22-31). He tells us to pray in faith, yet we doubt (James 1:5-8). He assures us that if we ask according to His will, *we will receive whatever* we ask for (Matt. 21:22). He cautions us, "Whoever trusts in his riches will fall," then He goes on to promise that, "the righteous will thrive like a green leaf" (Prov. 11:28). Yet many have succumbed to the lure of worldly pleasures and treasures, forsaking the riches of the heavenly kingdom that were meant for us all to enjoy.

In Matthew 4, while being tempted by Satan, Jesus, was offered, "all the kingdoms of the world and their splendor" (v. 8). However, Jesus stood fast on the Word of God and would not give in to the enemy's schemes. He knew that His Father alone was the source of true joy and fulfillment. In addition to observing Jesus' mastery in facing down temptation, we are given additional encouragement in 1 John 2:15-17:

> *Do not love the world or anything in the world. If anyone loves the world, the love of the Father is not in him. For everything in the world—the cravings of sinful man, the lust of his eyes and the boasting of what he has and does—comes not from the Father but from the world. The world and its desires pass away, but the man who does the will of God lives forever.*

In the case of the rich, young ruler, the young man earnestly desired to follow Jesus, but the cost of becoming a disciple was too high a price for him. His desire after the things of the world proved much greater than following the King of Kings.[105]

---

[105]Mark 10:17-22.

As we discussed previously, Solomon, the wisest and richest ruler in biblical times, was given a unique gift from the Lord: God was so well-pleased by his love, devotion, and sacrifices for Him that He told him that he could ask for anything he wanted. Solomon could have asked for any amount of worldly treasure under the sun. Instead, in all humility, he only asked that he would be endowed with wisdom to lead his people in a manner that would be pleasing to God and would benefit the people he served. In response, God generously answered his prayer, far beyond what he requested, by saying that He would also bless him with "both riches and honor" above any other ruler.[106]

We see here that Solomon had been given every earthly blessing imaginable, along with treasures from heaven. And yet, over time, because he turned away from God (indulging in lustful, worldly pleasures and practices), his life spiraled downward to a needless and heartbreaking end (1 Kings 11:9-12).

On the other hand, Job, another wealthy servant of the Lord, did nothing to deserve having everything most valuable taken from him. Still, when he did lose everything, he did not turn away, but turned to the Lord in his distress. The result of Job's obedience was God not only restoring, but also doubling Job's wealth (Job 42:12-17).

The comparison is glaringly obvious and staggering: God, in His sovereignty, can give and He can take away—sometimes with cause and sometimes with no apparent cause, to our human way of thinking. However, the profound lesson from this contrast is that

---

[106] 1 Kings 3:13.

those who are faithful to Him, who love Him, and follow His ways (no matter what they must endure in this life), are richly rewarded for all eternity (1 Pet. 1:3-9). The alternative is really not a viable alternative at all.

As we conclude our brief synopsis of the Ten Commandments, we come to understand that although some of them may be harder for us to keep than others, they are all of equal importance. We cannot exempt ourselves from obeying any of them—even if we feel like we can justify "fudging" on some, but not others (like lying or not fully honoring our parents). Schlessinger and Vogel put a fine point on this as they summarily state:

> When we violate one of the commandments, we disappoint God. We must see every act, both good and bad, as the one that tips the scales of judgment. It is through each act that God evaluates us and we evaluate ourselves.[107]

1. On the issue of sanctity of human life, what biblical defense can you make to someone who believes abortion and euthanasia are acceptable?

---

[107]Dr. Laura Schessinger and Rabbi Stewart Vogel, *The Ten Commandments: The Significance of God's Laws in Everyday Life* (Cliff Street Books/Harper Collins, 1998), pp. 20-21.

2. Consider the amount you currently tithe. Do you trust God completely to provide for your needs or do you find yourself tempted to fudge a little, in order to have some extra "insurance" or "fun money"?

3. Read Luke 12:15 and 1 Timothy 6:10. Compare with Philippians 4:12 and 1 Thessalonians 5:18. How can the right focus prevent covetousness?

CHAPTER 26

ORDINANCES

One Lord, one faith, one baptism.
Ephesians 4:5

Do this in remembrance of me.
1 Corinthians 11:24

A mong the many commands of the Lord we have been given, baptism and the Lord's Supper are two of the most significant. Jesus was our standard-bearer as He submitted to the Father's will when baptized by John the Baptist in the Jordan River (Matt. 3:13-17) and later on, when sharing the Last Supper with His disciples before His crucifixion (Luke 22:14-20).

Baptism

As John the Baptist paved the way for Jesus' earthly ministry, it was made clear that everyone seeking repentance must follow this command (Mark 1:4-5; Acts 19:4). Even so, there has been much controversy over the years with regard to the ordinance of baptism.

Some maintain that baptism is a condition for salvation, citing verses such as Mark 16:16 and 1 Peter 3:21 as proof positive. However, others believe that the Bible teaches that baptism is purely symbolic of dying to our old self and walking in newness of life in Christ (Rom. 6:3-6), as well as making a public declaration of faith in Christ (1 Cor. 12:13). The great theologian Charles Spurgeon once said, "A man who knows he is saved by believing in Christ does not, when he is baptized, lift his baptism into a saving ordinance. In fact, he is the very best protester against that mistake, because he holds that he has no right to be baptized until he is saved."

Numerous examples can be cited in the Bible of people who were saved, but not baptized. One case in point is the thief on the cross in Luke 23:39-43. Jesus' words in verse 43 make it indisputable that this man was ushered into the kingdom of God the day of his death. Yet clearly, there was no time for a baptismal service upon his acknowledging Jesus as his Savior, just prior to his passing. In addition, Abraham, Isaac, Jacob (among others of the Old Testament faithful), lived before the time that the ordinance of baptism was established. The fact that these worshippers of God were not baptized does not in any way negate that their salvation was sure.

Another point of contention on the matter of baptism is that many maintain that a person needs only to be sprinkled to be baptized, while others believe it is a biblical mandate that a person be immersed. The Greek word *"baptisma"* (noun) means "to submerge." When Jesus was baptized, we are told in Mark 1:10 that He "was coming up out of the water." Likewise, when the eunuch was baptized by Philip (Acts 8:39), he also "came up out of the water."

Beyond that, there are a number of verses in God's Word that validate this concept that baptism is intended to be by immersion alone. John 3:23 infers that baptizing where there is "plenty of water" is important. If you are being sprinkled, it is not vital to have a large quantity of water. Again, in Acts 8, it speaks of the eunuch "coming up out of the water" (vv. 36-39; see also a reference to Jesus in Mark 1:10). This emphasis on emerging out of a body of water does not lend itself well to the notion that one must only be sprinkled or have water poured on them. Further, the act of baptism is symboliac of our death and resurrection in Christ. To die, involves burial. To be resurrected denotes being raised to new life. This imagery is not consistent with the other two methods of baptism, as it would not be necessary to lower someone and then raise them up unless they were being submerged under the water.

Although many modern Lutheran churches today sprinkle or pour instead of submerge baptismal candidates, this was not always the case. Prior to this, the church held to the stance of its founder, as Martin Luther: "urged, in opposition to the standard practice of pouring, that baptism should be by immersion. He pointed out that the word in the Greek language means 'To plunge something entirely into the water, so that the water closes over it,' and urged that immersion should be the mode of baptism."[108]

---

[108]David E. Pratte, *Handbook of Religious Quotations, quoting A Compend of Luther's Theology, p. 167* (www.GospelWay.com), p. 11

Many can get caught up in heated theological debates over these issues, but what is most important is that, as believers, we try to "major on the majors" and not allow our differences in interpretations prevent us from being the unified Body of Christ we are called to be. We need to focus on the fact that we are in agreement that we must all follow Jesus' example to be baptized.

The Lord's Supper

A seminal moment in the relationship of Jesus with His disciples is that of the Last Supper. Jesus knew beforehand the importance of this meal as He instructed His disciples to make the necessary arrangements in preparation for this last major teachable moment with them before His arrest, trial, and crucifixion (Matt. 26:17-19). Once the preparations were made, the disciples soon discovered that this would not be an ordinary meal, like so many others they had enjoyed with their Master. For one thing, early on in the evening, Jesus revealed that one of them would betray Him. It was an incredulous thought to the disciples. Although they had disappointed Him, doubted Him, and didn't always understand Him, for the most part, they were devoted followers who loved Him, risked ridicule and worse for being associated with Him, and desired to become just like Him.

We are not talking groupies here. Many had followed Him, but had fallen away.[109] However, even though the disciples had trouble tracking with their Savior

---

[109]Matt. 19:22; Mark 15:6-14; John 6:66.

at times, they had spent enough time with Him (sitting under His teachings, taking note of the intimacy He shared with the Father, observing Him as He performed miracles, and watching as He demonstrated kindness, mercy, and humility), to know that He was indeed the Christ, the Son of God—the only path to eternal salvation. So when this appalling revelation was made known to them, they began to doubt their own allegiance to Jesus (v. 22).

We do well each time we celebrate the Lord's Supper to examine our own hearts and ask God to show us where we have failed him. Every time we disobey God, it is a form of betrayal in that we are choosing our way over His way, we are missing out on the privilege of exalting His holy name, and we are missing the mark in representing His character. Partaking of the Lord's Supper is a time for introspection. Yet it is never enough to simply recognize when we have disobeyed God. That is only the first step. We then must confess our sin and then repent of it. Finally, we must ask forgiveness. It is only then that our hearts can truly be prepared to receive the precious gift of communion.

In John 12, we are given yet another important lesson, as Jesus displays humility in washing the disciples' feet. Jesus' mastery in storytelling is legendary. However, His leading by example was an especially effective way of conveying life-changing truth. As we contemplate the sacrifice Jesus made for us, we need to also reflect on our encounters with others in recent times and examine our hearts to see if we have been modeling Christlike humility. God is always faithful to bring to mind specific people who we may have offended and from whom we may need to ask forgiveness.

Pastors often reinforce this principle during the Lord's Supper as they remind their congregations of the admonition found in Matthew 5:23-24. We cannot on one hand, be reverent before the Lord at the communion table, while at the same time be flippant about our offenses toward others. Paul expresses this so well in Acts 24:16 as he professes to "strive *always* to keep [his] conscience clear before God and man" (*emphasis mine*).

Once again, we are faced with a word that packs a punch. We can easily gloss right over the word "*always*" and trick our minds into thinking that it is enough to strive *often* or strive *occasionally*. Even though we no longer live under the age of law, God requires us to strive toward obeying His law to the full extent of our capability *by His grace*. No excuses. No watering down His message. No deluding ourselves into thinking that our disobedience doesn't matter to Him.

Every aspect of the Lord's Supper is as relevant for us today as it was for the disciples back then. Whether we come to the altar with a pure heart or a heart that is in need of cleansing, we must take this time of remembrance seriously. The soul-cleansing, life-giving, redeeming act of Jesus shedding His blood for our sins may be once-and-for-all time, but the very nature of that timeless act demands our ongoing and utmost praise, adoration, thanksgiving, and penitent hearts laid bare and fully yielded to Him.

We can look forward to the day when we will celebrate together with Him in the marriage feast of the Lamb. In the meantime, however, we must honor Him by continuing to reflect on what He has already done through His great sacrifice for us.

1. What does baptism symbolize? Why do you think it was important for Jesus to be baptized? Why do you think it is important for believers to be baptized?

2. What is the purpose of believers corporately celebrating the Lord's Supper? How does remembering Christ's sacrifice for you deepen your walk with Him?

CONCLUSION

May God himself, the God of peace, sanctify
you through and through. May your whole
spirit, soul and body be kept blameless at
the coming of our Lord Jesus Christ. The one
who calls you is faithful and he will do it.
                                    1 Thessalonians 5:23-24

My primary motivation for writing this book was to encourage in each of us a growing passion for God, a greater hunger for His Word, and a deepening desire to love others with the transforming love of Jesus. We are meant to cheer each other on until we all cross the finish line and hear our Master say, "Well done!"

As I've prayed over and written these words, I have tried to represent the truth of God's Word accurately and authentically. I have also sought to be transparent, as I've shared about living out my Christian faith. I don't always get it right, but I've come a long ways...knowing that I still have a ways to go. I look forward to the day that I am perfected in eternity, but I take heart in every victory God has given me so far toward that end.

I hope that as you've turned these pages (observing our perfect teacher, Jesus, and identifying with many less-than-perfect characters in both the Bible and modern role models, and "listening" as I've shared my own struggles and victories along the way), that you have been challenged to go deeper and farther with God than ever before.

God did not promise that our life in Him on this earth would be all sunshine and roses. We can rest assured though, that every bit of effort, pain, or loss will pale in light of eternal glory.

I pray that God will give each of us the courage and confidence to meet the challenge of obeying all the commands He has given us to obey. Be patient...for He certainly is! And as we continue to seek to obey God fully, we can rest in this promise:

The LORD will fulfill his purpose for me.
Psalm 138:8

Appendix 1

Abbreviated Concordance of God's Promises and Commands

GOD'S PART (Some key promise verses containing the words "all" "always," or "every"):

<u>"All"/"Always" verses</u>:

But seek first his kingdom and his righteousness, and all these things will be given to you as well (Matt. 6:33).

But the Counselor, the Holy Spirit, whom the Father will send in my name, will teach you all things and will remind you of everything I have said to you (Jn. 14:26— See also Jn. 16:13).

And we know that in all things God works for the good of those who love him, who have been called according to his purpose" (Rom. 8:28).

In all these things we are more than conquerors through him who loved us (Rom. 8:37).

But thanks be to God, who always leads us in triumphal procession in Christ and through us spreads everywhere the fragrance of the knowledge of him (2 Cor. 2:14).

God is able to make all grace abound to you, so that in all things at all times, having all that you need, you will abound in every good work (2 Cor. 9:8).

To him who is able to do immeasurably more than all we ask or imagine, according to his power that is at work within us to him be glory in the church and in Christ Jesus throughout all generations, for ever and ever! Amen (Eph. 3:21).

And my God will meet all your needs according to his glorious riches in Christ Jesus (Phil. 4:19).

But if we walk in the light, we have fellowship with one another, and the blood of Jesus, his Son, purifies us from all sin (1 Jn. 1:7).

If we confess our sins, he is faithful and just and will forgive us our sins and purify us from all unrighteousness (1 Jn. 1:9).

"Every"/"Everything" Verses:

You know with all your heart and soul that not one of all the good promises the LORD your God gave you has failed. Every promise has been fulfilled; not one has failed (Josh. 23:14).

For the Lord searches every heart and understands every motive behind the thoughts (1 Chron. 28:9).

Every Word of God is flawless; he is a shield to those who take refuge in him (Prov. 30:5).

He has made everything beautiful in its time (Eccl. 3:11).

His compassions never fail. They are new every morning (Lam. 3:22-23).

His divine power has given us everything we need for life and godliness through our knowledge of him who called us by his own glory and goodness (2 Pet. 1:3-4).

OUR PART: (Some key commandment verses containing "All" "Always," and "Every"):

Love the LORD your God with all your heart and with all your soul and with all your strength" (Deut. 6:5). Trust in the Lord with all your heart and lean not on your own understanding; in all your ways acknowledge him, and he will make your paths straight (Prov. 3:5-6). Therefore go and make disciples of all nations, baptizing them in the name of the Father and of the Son and of the Holy Spirit, and teaching them to obey everything I have commanded you. And surely I am with you always, to the very end of the age (Matt. 28-19-20).

Always give yourselves fully to the work of the Lord, because you know that your labor in the Lord is not in vain (1 Cor. 15:58).

Be joyful always (1 Thess. 5:17).

Give thanks in all circumstances, for this is God's will for you in Christ Jesus (1 Thess. 5:18).

Cast all your anxiety on him because he care for you (1 Pet. 5:7).

PART 2: Scripture references for specific commandments)

Abide: Ps. 37:7, 46:10; Jn. 15:4-5,7, 9;
           Gal. 2:20; Col. 2:6; 1 Jn. 2:6, 24, 27, 28,
           3:24; 2 Jn. 1:9.

Confess: Lev. 5:5; Jas. 4:8, 5:16; 1 Jn. 1:9.

Encourage: Rom. 14:19; 1 Thess. 5:11; Heb. 10:24.

Forgive: Lk. 6:38; Eph. 4:32; Col. 3:13.

Gratitude: Ps. 95:2, 107:1, 136:26; Eph. 5:20; Col.
           3:15; 1 Thess. 5:18.

Holiness: 2 Cor. 7:1; 1 Pet. 1:15-16.

Humility: Eph. 4:2; Jas. 4:10; 1 Pet. 5:5-6.

Joy: Ps. 118:24; Prov. 17:22; Hab. 3:18; 1
           Thess. 5:16; Jas. 1:2.

Justice: Lev. 19:15; Deut. 32:4; Ps. 33:5, 140:12;
           Isa. 1:17, 9:7, 30:18, 51:4-5, 61:8;
           Mic. 6:8; Lk. 18:7; Acts 17:31; Heb. 9:27;
           Rev. 19:11.

Love: Lev. 19:18; Deut. 6:5; Matt. 5:44;
             Mk. 12:30; Jn. 13:35, 15:12-13, 17;
             Rom 12:9-13; 1 Cor. 13:4-8, 16:14;
             Gal. 5:14; Col. 3:14; 1 Pet.1:22, 4:8;
             1 Jn. 4:11-12, 3:18.

Meditate: Josh. 1:8; Job 22:22, 37:14; Ps. 77:12,
             107:43, 119:15-16, 97; 143:5, 145:5;
             Phil. 4:8; Col. 3:1-2.

Memorize: Ps. 119:11; Prov. 2:1-6.

Mercy: Ps. 23:6, 25:6, 145:9, 146:8; Lam 3:22,
             Mic. 6:8; Matt. 5:7, 9:13; Lk. 1:50, 6:36;
             Rom. 9:15-16; Eph. 2:4; Tit. 3:5; Heb.
             4:16; Jas. 2:13; 1 Pet. 1:3; Jude 1:22-23.

Obey: Gen. 17:1; Deut. 5:32, 6:18, 11:1;
             Josh. 22:5; Jn. 14:15, 23, 15:10;
             Rev. 3:3.

Peace: Rom. 12:18; 2 Cor. 13:11; Heb. 12:14;
             1 Pet. 3:11.

Pray: 2 Chron. 7:14; Lk. 11:9; Jn. 16:24;
             Col. 4:2; 1 Thess. 5:17; Jas. 5:13-14.

Repent: Matt. 4:17; Acts 3:19; Rev. 3:3.

Serve: 1 Sam. 12:20; 1 Chron. 28:9; Ps. 100:2;
             Matt. 25:40; Gal. 6:10; Eph. 6:7; 1 Pet.
             4:10-11.

Seek: 1 Chron. 28:9; Ps. 105:4; Isa. 55:6;
             Matt. 6:33.

Share: Matt. 25:40; Rom. 12:13; 1 Pet. 4:9;
1 Jn. 3:17.

Study: Prov. 4:13; Matt. 4:4; Acts 17:11;
Rom. 15:4; 2 Tim. 2:15, 3:16-17;
1 Pet. 3:15.

Submit: Ps. 37:5; Prov. 16:3; Eph. 5:21;
Jas. 4:7-8; 1 Pet. 2:13.

Testify: Matt. 28:19-20; Mk. 16:15; 1 Cor. 1:17;
2 Cor. 5:20; 2 Tim. 4:2; Heb. 12:15; 1
Pet. 3:15.

Trust: Ps. 37:3, 5, 7; Ps. 62:8; Prov. 3:5-6.

Unity: 1 Cor. 1:10, 2 Cor. 13:11; Eph. 4:3;
Phil. 2:2.

Do Not's:

Fear: Josh. 1:9; Isa. 35:4, 41:10, 43:1, 13;
Jer. 1:8.

Judge: Matt. 7:1; Lk. 6:37-38; 1 Cor. 4:5;
Jas. 4:11.

Other: Ps. 4:4; Ps. 103:2-5, 146:3; Prov. 3:7, 27, 25:9, 30:6; Matt. 5:39, 6:25, 31; Jn. 6:27, 14:1, 27; Rom. 6:12, 12:2, 3, 14, 16-17, 19, 21; 1 Cor. 10:7- 10; 2 Cor. 2:17, 4:16-17, 6:14; Gal. 6:7, 9; Eph. 4:29, 30, 5:18; Phil. 4:6; Col. 3:9; 1 Thess. 5:19- 20; 1 Tim. 4:12, 14; 2 Tim. 2:23; Heb. 10:35- 36, 13:16; Jas. 1:22, 5:9, 12; 1 Pet 3:9, 4:12; 1 Jn. 2:15; 1 Jn. 4:13; Jn. 11.

Appendix 2

RESOURCES

Apologetics:

Evidence That Demands a Verdict (Josh McDowell, Here's Life Publishers/Campus Crusade for Christ, 1972).

Know What You Believe (Paul E. Little, Victor Books, 1987).

Know Why You Believe (Paul E. Little, Cook Communications/Victor, 1999).

Ready With An Answer (John Ankerberg/John Weldon, Harvest House Publishers, 1997).

Reasons Skeptics Should Consider Christianity (Josh McDowell/Don Stewart, Living Books/Tyndale House Publishers, 1986).

The Case for Christ (Lee Strobel, Zondervan, 1998).

The Questions Christians Hope No One Will Ask (Mark Mittelberg, Tyndale House Publishers, 2010).

Why Believe? (Greg Laurie, Tyndale House Publishers, 1995).

Bible Study Methods:

Discover the Bible for Yourself: (Kay Arthur/Precept Ministries, Harvest House Publishers, 2000).

How To Enjoy the Boring Parts of the Bible (Philip Rosenbaum, Wolgemuth & Hyatt, Publishers, Inc. 1991).

How to Study the Bible and Enjoy It (Skip Heitzig, Tyndale House Publishers, Inc., 2002).

How to Read the Bible for All Its Worth: A Guide To Understanding the Bible: (Gordon D. Fee/Douglas Stuart (Academie Books/Zondervan, 1982).

Living by the Book (Howard G. Hendricks/William D. Hendricks, Moody Press, 1991).

Playing with Fire: How the Bible Ignites Change in Your Soul (Walt Russell, NavPress, 2000).

Rick Warren's Bible Study Methods: Twelve Ways You Can Unlock God's Word: (Rick Warren, Zondervan, 2006).

Talk Thru the Bible (Bruce Wilkinson/Kenneth Boa, Thomas Nelson Publishers, 1983).

Understanding and Applying the Bible (J. Robertson McQuilkin, Moody Press, 1983).

What the Bible is All About (Henrietta Mears, Regal Books/ Gospel Light Publications, 2011).

Discipleship Aids:

Celebration of Discipline (Richard J. Foster, Harper San Francisco, 1988).

Discipleship Essentials: A Guide to Building Your Life in Christ (Greg Ogden, InterVarsity Press, 2007).

Spiritual Disciplines for the Christian (Donald Whitney, NavPress, 1991).

The Complete Book of Discipleship: (Bill Hull, NavPress, 2006).

The Cost of Discipleship (Dietrich Bonhoeffer, The MacMillan Co., 1966).

What on Earth Am I Here For? (Rick Warren, Zondervan, 2012—formerly titled, *"The Purpose Driven Life"*).

With Christ in the School of Disciple Building (Carl Wilson, Zondervan Publishing House, 1976).

Evangelism:

How to Share Your Faith (Greg Laurie, Tyndale Publishers, Inc. 1999).

Becoming a Contagious Christian (Bill Hybels and Mark Mittelberg, Zondervan, 1994).

Joining Jesus On His Mission: How to Be an Everyday Missionary (Greg Finke, TenthPower Publishing, 2014).

One Thing You Can't Do in Heaven (Mark Cahill, Biblical Discipleship Publishers, 2005).

Tell Someone (Greg Laurie, B & H Publishing Group, 2016).

The Way of the Master (Ray Comfort, Bridge-Logos, 2006).

Witnessing Without Fear (Bill Bright, Here's Life Publishers, 1987).

Online Resources:

Answers in Genesis (www.answersingenesis.org).

Apologetics Resource Center (www.arcapologetics.org).

Bible Resources (www.bibleresources.org).

Christian Answers (www.christiananswers.net).

Creation Ministries International (www.creation.com).

Creation Research Society (www.creationresearch.org).

Probe for Answers (www.probe.org).

Summit Ministries (www.summit.org).

TargetTruthMinistries (Gerry Burney, www.targettruthministries.com).

The Bible Project (Tim Mackie/Jon Collins & Team, www.bibleproject.com).